BANKING ON THE STATE

Finance Matters

Series Editors: Kathryn Lavelle, *Case Western Reserve University, Cleveland, Ohio* and Timothy J. Sinclair, *University of Warwick*

This series of books provides advanced introductions to the processes, relationships and institutions that make up the global financial system. Suitable for upper-level undergraduate and taught graduate courses in financial economics and the political economy of finance and banking, the series explores all aspects of the workings of the financial markets within the context of the broader global economy.

Published

Banking on the State: The Political Economy of Public Savings Banks
Mark K. Cassell

The European Central Bank
Michael Heine and Hansjörg Herr

Quantitative Easing: The Great Central Bank Experiment
Jonathan Ashworth

BANKING ON THE STATE

The Political Economy of Public Savings Banks

MARK K. CASSELL

agenda
publishing

© Mark K. Cassell 2021

First published in 2021 by Agenda Publishing

Agenda Publishing Limited
The Core
Bath Lane
Newcastle Helix
Newcastle upon Tyne
NE4 5TF

www.agendapub.com

ISBN 978-1-78821-195-6 (hardcover)
ISBN 978-1-78821-196-3 (paperback)

British Library Cataloguing-in-Publication Data
A catalogue record for this book is available from the British Library

Typeset in Warnock Pro by Patty Rennie
Printed and bound in the UK by CPI Group (UK) Ltd, Croydon, CR0 4YY

For Kurt Moosdorf

CONTENTS

PREFACE

I spent summers as a young child and teenager living with my grandparents in an enchanting, small town called Büdingen, located an hour's drive from the metropolis of Frankfurt. Each summer, I was transported from the strip malls of southern California to the small forest-covered region of postwar West Germany. Büdingen was the county seat, and my grandfather, Kurt Moosdorf, served as county executive or Landrat, for more than 25 years. As Landrat, my grandfather oversaw local government, including the economic development and public infrastructure projects that were part of Germany's postwar economic miracle.

My grandparents' house overlooked the local Sparkasse. The Sparkasse was often the first stop my grandmother and I made each morning on our grocery-shopping rounds. She would chat with the staff, check her account, or pick up a deposit receipt. It seemed normal for her to know everyone in the bank. Several decades later, I realized the reason she knew everyone at the Sparkasse was that her husband, the Landrat, was the first line of supervision and governance in Germany's public savings banks. My grandfather chaired the supervisory board of Büdingen's Sparkasse for more than two decades, and it was my grandfather who oversaw the banks' construction.

When I visited the Sparkasse in Büdingen in 2018, I learned it had merged and become part of a larger county system. The building was newer, the layout was different, and ATMs dotted the lobby. The name and brand were similar though: a giant recognizable red "S" with a dot over the top. I wanted to know how this institution, which had played such a central role in my grandfather's life and the life of Germany, had evolved and developed. It seemed to be thriving and I wondered why. How could a small local financial institution, governed and overseen by local politicians no less, survive global capitalism and privatization? What was going on?

Politics is another driver for this book. Three recent global challenges underscore Sparkassen's significance. The first is the Great Recession of 2007/08. For more than 200 years, Sparkassen have been at the centre of Germany's model of capitalism. The global recession taught us that history does not predict the future. Sparkassen's long history does not guarantee their future. The financial crisis in the 2000s hurt Germany's economy and undermined trust in the country's financial system. Yet, Sparkassen stayed away from the opaque and risky investments that brought down the global economy. Local savings banks also kept credit flowing to firms and families during and after the financial crisis.

Second, during the refugee crisis in 2015/16, millions of refugees from Africa, the Middle East, and Central Asia poured into Europe. Most credit institutions denied refugees banking accounts because they lacked identification. This was a major problem for refugees and Germany's local governments who rely on bank transfers to provide social assistance. Sparkassen rose to the challenge: giving hundreds of thousands of refugees access to credit, a safe place to keep their assets, and ways for local governments to provide social assistance when it was needed most.

Finally, as the book was being completed, Sparkassen were playing a central role in the federal government's response to the economic downturn caused by the Covid-19 pandemic. Germany passed a €750 billion aid package to stabilize the economy in March 2020, €600 billion of subsidized loans to businesses. Small and medium-sized enterprises, the backbone of Germany's economy, applied for the federal aid through credit institutions, primarily Sparkassen. In the United States, businesses also applied for federal assistance through banks. However, US banks were mainly private commercial banks and widely criticized for adopting policies that favoured large companies (with larger fees) over small businesses. Sparkassen, by contrast, lobbied on behalf of their small-business customers to ensure aid reached Germany's SMEs on time.

The Great Recession, the refugee crisis, and Covid-19 underscore Germany's local savings banks' important political role today. They are for-profit entities that also serve the public interest. While my grandfather's connection made me aware of Sparkassen, it was their role in the recent global challenges that prompted this research. How was such a system sustainable? How were Sparkassen able to avoid the risky behaviour and corruption that plagued private banks? How had the institution my grandfather used to rebuild his community in the aftermath of the Second World War adjusted to a world of global finance, European integration, digitalization, and the wake of the financial crisis?

In short, the book is motivated by a single simple question: what explains Germany's public savings banks?

The book is written for several readerships. Scholars interested in the role credit and finance play in Germany's economic model will appreciate a book that offers a clear and concise account of Sparkassen. There is a robust literature on financialization and Germany's model of capitalism that includes comparative political economists, economic sociologists, and German studies scholars. However, with the notable exceptions of Reinhard Schmidt, Richard Deeg, Christoph Scherrer, Oliver Butzbach, and Kurt von Mettenheim, few scholars have written about Germany's public savings banks and their role in Germany's economic system for an English-speaking audience.

Public administration scholars are the second readership. Sparkassen constitute unique hybrid institutions that combine elements of the private and public sectors. As such, Sparkassen share administrative elements and challenges of government sponsored enterprises (GSEs), quasi-governmental organizations (Quangos), and special authorities. This book's central contribution is a clear explanation of how Germany harnesses what are typically private entities and private markets in the pursuit of public interests; what are the accountability and governance mechanisms that keep Sparkassen focused on their public mission? How is administration a comparative advantage? These issues are at the centre of public administration. *Banking on the State* builds on the work of scholars such as Donald Kettl, Anne Khademian, Susan Hoffmann, Reinhard Schmidt, Wolfgang Seibel, Jonathan Koppel, and Thomas Stanton.

Finally, this book is written for the growing number of scholars, activists, and US policymakers interested in establishing an American version of Sparkassen. The Bank of North Dakota is America's only public bank. It is successful and surprisingly popular in one of the most conservative states in the nation. A growing number of states – California, New Mexico, New Jersey, Washington – are actively considering public banks modelled, in part, on Germany's Sparkassen. This book seeks to contribute to those promoting and developing more public banks in the United States.

*   *   *

The method used in this work is known as "grounded" research (Glaser & Strauss 2009; Hoffmann & Cassell 2010). Pioneered by Anselm Strauss, grounded theory seeks to explain and theorize using field data and experiential data. Field data include a range of materials from the field: notes of observations, transcripts of interviews, visual materials such as art or photos, and documents. Experiential data – "data in the head" of a researcher – includes bodies of social science literature, life experiences that are germane, and professional experiences. These lead to insights, hypotheses, and questions that are verified with field data.

The emphasis on data does not mean the research is entirely inductive. Grounded researchers like James Q. Wilson, Herbert Kaufman, and John Dewey, emphasize the interplay among induction, deduction, and empirical verification in developing an understanding of a social phenomenon like Sparkassen and generating theory. I build on the insights of James Q. Wilson to explain the resilience of Sparkassen from the perspective of the operators, managers, and executives in the organization as well as the institutional actors and competitors outside the organizations (Wilson 2000). The process begins with a "generative question". In this study, the generative question was: "What explains Germany's public sector savings banks' resilience?" The question was triggered by an earlier investigation of the failure of regional public banks and the surprising success of Sparkassen during the financial crisis.

According to Strauss, after developing a generative question, the researcher gathers and analyzes field data. Field data analysis starts with "coding" and "memoing". In coding, the researcher searches the data for categories, or concepts, and relationships among the categories. "Axial coding" looks for subcategories, essentially dimensions of the concept. I use NVivo, a qualitative data processing software, to code interview data and other documents, extracting passages that cover similar concepts. Memo writing occurs when data analysis is underway. Memos are used to suggest a hypothesis, add clarity, make connections, and raise questions. In this study, memos take the form of annotations within the coding process.

Grounded theory is an iterative process. The researcher collects field data, codes it, and returns to the field for additional data and to the library for additional literature. In this study, an initial round of interviews was conducted in 2014 with public and private banking officials, federal regulators, Sparkassen managers, and journalists and academics writing about the financial crisis. It was this initial set of interviews that led to the generative question that informed the research. Based on the first collection of interviews and data collected, I designed additional interviews, collected documentary data from government sources, and read additional periodic and scholarly work on Sparkassen. According to Strauss, the grounded theory that results from the iterative process is conceptually dense and reflects the assumption that the social world is complex, and relationships are often contingent.

In 2018–19, I conducted a second round of semi-structured interviews with managers, executives, and politicians managing Sparkassen, including those in the regional and federal associations. Four banks were selected based on two criteria: size (large and small) and location (East vs West). The size of an institution was identified as significant in earlier interviews with bank officials and the broader literature on banking. Larger banks are assumed to have more power, resources, and tools than smaller institutions. At the same time, larger institutions often face higher expectations and more significant challenges than smaller institutions. The East vs West criteria were also triggered by interviews and scholarship. Despite the unification of East and West Germany in 1989, the country remains deeply divided. Eastern regions are poorer and economically weaker than their western counterparts. Although Sparkassen existed in East Germany before 1989, their relationship with the local community was significantly different from that in West Germany. To tap into a broad range of experiences, I selected one large and one small Sparkasse in the east and one large and one small Sparkasse in the west.

Interviews with managers and supervisory board members of particular Sparkassen shed light on how internal governance structures and external regulatory frameworks shaped Sparkassen's investment behaviours during the financial crisis and on the value Sparkassen contribute to local governments and communities.

Second, I interviewed leaders from Deutsche Sparkassen- und Giroverband (DSGV), the trade association for Germany's Sparkassen. The DSGV serves two essential roles. As the formal representative of Sparkassen interests in Germany and Brussels, the DSGV leadership explains the political and policy debates surrounding the EU banking union, particularly the efforts to adopt a single European-wide depository insurance scheme. In cooperation with regional Sparkassen associations, the DSGV also plays a role in the governance and strategy of Sparkassen, helping make sense of the institutional arrangements that hold Sparkassen accountable. As the primary representative for Sparkassen at the national and EU level, the DSGV sheds light on the European Commission's politics over the banking union.

I also interviewed institutional actors including staff to Members of the European Parliament (MEP) who served on the Committee on Economic and Monetary Affairs (ECON) during the time banking union legislation was debated; public banking interest groups; private banking interest groups; representatives of cooperative banks; and federal regulators in the Bundesbank and the BaFin. I visited over a dozen Sparkassen throughout eastern and western parts of the country, spent time observing how they operated and spoke with dozens of commercial and individual customers who bank with Sparkassen.

Secondary sources of field data supplement my findings. These include German auditing reports, legislative hearing documentation produced by the German federal government and several state governments and reports produced by the European Union. I also rely on financial data from the DSGV and the Eastern Regional Sparkassen Association. These detail the location, size, and fiscal performance of Sparkassen across the country over time. And finally, a good deal of information derives from accounts from journalists and scholars.

ACKNOWLEDGEMENTS

Any errors and mistakes in this book rest squarely with the author. However, I could not have completed this project without incurring several significant debts. Conversations with Horst Gischer Michael Schwan, Richard Deeg, Shawn Donnelly, Jonas Markgraf, Elliot Posner, Rachel Epstein, Martin Rhodes, Wolfram Morales, Mirko Weis, Sigurt Vitols, and Kathryn Lavelle were invaluable in helping hone my arguments. I am indebted to the US and German Fulbright Commissions for the financial support that enabled me to conduct the first round of interviews. I also owe a debt of gratitude to the Wissenschaftszentrum Berlin für Sozialforschung (WZB) for giving me the opportunity to connect and interact with some of the smartest social scientists on the planet. Also, this book would not have been comprehensible without the help of Amy Hanauer, William Cassell, Alison Howson, who helped cull much of the jargon and academic prose. Finally, I wish to thank the anonymous reviewers for their thoughtful and helpful suggestions.

In addition, this research would not have been possible without the willingness of dozens of respondents to share their perspectives and insights into Sparkassen. It is their stories and experiences that form the basis for this book. *Dankeschön*!

Mark K. Cassell

TABLES AND FIGURES

Tables

Figures

1
INTRODUCTION

"Public banks like Sparkassen shouldn't really exist in a capitalist system"
– Manager at a German private commercial bank.

Germany's public savings banks, known as Sparkassen, present a three-fold puzzle for today's world of global capitalism. First, Sparkassen – relatively small financial institutions with comparatively few assets – are nonetheless the economic engines that drive Europe's largest economy. Sparkassen are the most important source of capital for consumers and small- and medium-sized enterprises in Germany, a country whose high-skill, export-based economy is built on small- and medium-sized enterprises. Sparkassen account for 43 per cent of all business lending (Simpson 2013), 70 per cent of lending to self-employed and trades, and more than half of all consumer lending (Deutsche Bundesbank 2020). No other advanced industrialized country in the world – let alone one with an economy as large as Germany's – relies as much on such small public institutions to fuel its economy.

A second puzzling aspect of Sparkassen is that their recent experience contradicts two key narratives in comparative political economy and international political economy: that global pressures and ascendance of neoliberal ideas will lead to the demise of Germany's unique form of capitalism and that in an era of global financial capitalism, competitive pressures force banks to grow in size and breadth (see Schmidt 2018). Smaller financial institutions lack the capital and know-how to compete; Sparkassen should be relics of the past. Yet, Sparkassen remain a central part of the German model. They embody the country's ordoliberal economic ideas and democratic principles of self-governance. In contrast to classical liberalism or neoliberalism, ordoliberals promotes a strong role for the state in the maintenance of a social market economy. However, the state is a rule-setting state (Blyth 2013: 146). Ordoliberalism views the state's role to establish a legal arena that maintains healthy competition, adheres to market principles, and lets market actors regulate themselves (Campbell & Lindberg 1990;

Smyser 1993). In this sense ordoliberalism stands in contrast to libertarian or neoliberal ideas of economic freedom as unfettered competition with limited state involvement (Gook 2018). While the public savings banks face significant challenges from low interest rates, efforts by the European Union to standardize banking regulation, and global competition, Sparkassen continue to provide liquidity even as the larger commercial banks and state-level public banks known as Landesbanken consolidate or close. Between 2006 and 2009, new loans made by Sparkassen to businesses increased 46 per cent from €42.5 billion to €62.1 billion (Simpson 2013: 4). Even during the worst period of the financial crisis in 2007/08 when most banks curtailed their lending, Sparkassen continued to lend to start-up firms; providing loans to an average of 7,000 new start-ups each year between 2006 and 2009.[1]

Sparkassen's performance during the recent financial crisis raises the third puzzle. During the Great Recession of 2007–08, larger private and public institutions in Germany, the United States and elsewhere gambled on mortgage-backed securities (MBS) and derivative products and lost (von Mettenheim & Butzbach 2012; von Mettenheim 2012). Smaller public savings banks in countries like Spain also suffered from losses, greed and corruption. Moreover, as universal banks, Sparkassen could have expanded their investment banking activities to risky derivative markets. However, in contrast to larger public and private institutions, and smaller public banks in other countries like Spain, Sparkassen opted to keep their business focus on lending within their regions. As a result, Sparkassen avoided losses during the financial crisis and continued to earn steady returns even at the peak of the recession in 2008.

In short, Germany's public savings banks are an enigma in today's global capitalism and their experience prompts a relatively simple set of questions at the centre of this book: How have Sparkassen managed to adapt and survive the economic turmoil and global pressures of the past several decades? What enable these small public eighteenth-century financial institutions to remain at the centre of Germany's system of finance? In this period when "too big to fail" and neoliberal ideas seem ascendant, how have Germany's Sparkassen managed global pressures and continued to flourish? With the exception of several scholars (Schmidt *et al.* 2014; Butzbach & von Mettenheim 2014; Butzbach 2008) Sparkassen's resilience in the face of domestic and global pressures has received relatively little attention despite their central place in the country's economy and the scholarly attention devoted to banking and finance more generally in Germany.

Germany is the most prominent example of a bank-based system of capitalism (along with Japan) (Albert 1993). The country's banking system is the centrepiece of some of the most seminal works in comparative political economy (Gerschenkron 1989; Shonfield 1969; Zysman 1994). These classic works spawned a second generation of scholarship by political economists (Deeg 1999; Hardie *et al.* 2013), economists (Krahnen & Schmidt 2004); and sociologists (Vitols 1998, 2005) that describe in depth the institutional complexities and functions of Germany's banking system. The financial crisis of 2007/08 and the European debt crisis triggered another generation of scholars who sought to make sense of the crisis, its impact on Germany's banks, and the European Union's growing role shaping the context within which banks operate (Deeg & Hardie 2016; Hardie & Thompson 2020). There is a robust literature, for example, on why German private and large public state banks suffered loses. Explanations typically centre on poor decision making on the part of bank managers, insufficient regulatory oversight (particularly regarding cross-border operations), a lack of a functioning business plan, and policies by the EU that reduced the involvement of government in the banking sector.

Missing from the large literature on German and European banking is an explanation for why Germany's public savings banks continue to survive and thrive even as similar banks in nearly every other advanced industrialized country have struggled, transformed, or disappeared.

There is a strong literature on bank failures and banking crises (Black 2013; Barth *et al.*; United States 2011). Deregulation, poor management, too much regulation, incompetence, greed – these are just a sample of causes cited for why banks fail. But why do they succeed and thrive? Is it the lack of greed? Greater competence? Regulation? Lack of regulation? Most analyses of banking performance share an underlying market assumption that if banks succeed and thrive it is because they performed better, showed more effective leadership, made better choices, developed strategic plans, hired more competent and ethical managers, or simply got lucky. While this book does not disagree with many of the explanations for why banks fall into receivership, the reasons often cited are incomplete.

In the case of Sparkassen, it is difficult to argue that the CEOs of 385 credit institutions are more ethical or more competent or showed greater leadership skills than CEOs of savings banks in other countries, or the CEOs of large private and public banks in Germany. Certainly, Sparkassen made better choices than German Landesbanken or the big four commercial banks (Deutsche Bank, Commerzbank, IKB Deutsche Industriebank and Dresdner Bank) but the more interesting question is why? What kept Sparkassen from making the poor choices that landed private banks and regional public banks into trouble? And more broadly, what explains the resilience of Sparkassen even as public savings banks in other countries disappear or are in decline? This book argues that the explanation for why credit institutions like Sparkassen succeed is more complicated and, arguably, more interesting than what scholars and practitioners have presented.

The answer developed in this book is three-fold. The first is economic. Despite expectations to the contrary, Sparkassen remain successful because of the particular economic value they provide the country. In contrast to private banks, state banking laws limit the territory in which a Sparkassen can do business to a relatively small area – typically a city or county. This so-called "regional principle" is an institutional design feature that ensures a public savings bank has a strong incentive to promote its region's economic health. Sparkassen promote the economic health directly and indirectly: direct lending to local and regional governments, SMEs, and low- and medium-income households that other banks undersupply; and indirectly, by being at the centre of a regional economic network, strengthening the capacity of local economic actors, and channelling excess reserves to civic and economic institutions that further strengthen the social capital of a region.

Organization is the second part of the explanation for Sparkassen's resilience. Although the 385 Sparkassen operate and are governed independently of one another, they are part of a large banking network known as the Finanzgruppe Deutscher Sparkassen- und Giroverband or "S-Group". The S-Group network consists of federal state banks (Landesbanken), building societies, insurance companies, an IT company, and numerous other financial service providers. The network plays an essential role in boosting the capacity of public savings banks; enabling small credit institutions to benefit from a number of economies of scale that large credit institutions have. At the same time, the networks, as well as each savings bank's organization, contribute to accountability and oversight. A Sparkasse is governed by multiple and overlapping oversight committees including supervisory boards, credit committees, monitoring committees and transparency committees. The web of oversight creates a system of checks and balances that support stability at a relatively low cost. Sparkassen are also insured by 11 regional institutional protection insurance funds which form a joint-liability scheme. Meaning, each savings bank contributes to a fund covering all Sparkassen. The funds serve as the first line of defence in an institutional protection scheme while simultaneously fulfilling the legal deposit insurance responsibility. In keeping with Germany's ordoliberal approach to regulatory policy, the shared liability incentivizes savings banks to regulate themselves; to prevent an individual savings bank from going rogue by, for example, betting on complicated financial products. The insurance system directly insures institutions rather than depositors. By insuring creditors, the bank insurance system creates an incentive for local economic actors to do business with the savings banks. At the same time, the system places Sparkassen at the centre of a network of banking relationships built on patient capital and coordinated economic policy.

A third and final part of the explanation for the Sparkassen's role in Germany's economy is politics. Sparkassen remain one of the most politically powerful economic sectors in Germany. Represented by the Deutscher Sparkassen- und Giroverband (DSGV) at the federal level and 12 regional associations, public savings banks' power stems from several sources including: (1) geographic distribution, the 385 independent savings banks with 13,000 branches are located in nearly every town and city in Germany; (2) close connection to citizens and voters, more than half of all citizens have their savings accounts with Sparkassen and surveys show the public holds Sparkassen in high trust; (3) Sparkassen's place within the large S-Group banking network; and more importantly, (4) Sparkassen's relationship with local political and economic leaders. Many of the country's policymakers served or continue to serve on the supervisory boards of Sparkassen. If all politics is local, Sparkassen are the nation's power players. Their influence enables Sparkassen to maintain their institutional character, protect their interests, and confront national reforms and European Union efforts that weaken them.

The Great Recession of 2007/08 generated a cottage industry of tales of extraordinary malfeasance by "Too big to fail" institutions. Popular books, movies and podcasts[2] capture these stories of casino capitalism gone awry: big institutions leveraging their equity to take advantage of implicit state guarantees; exotic and complicated assets that only the most sophisticated mathematicians can understand; and government regulators complacent, coopted or overwhelmed. In our focus on "Too Big To Fail" we miss a story that is just as compelling, just as surprising, and – like the financial autopsies of the Lehman Brothers of the world – offers lessons for how to think about banking and finance in the future.

Finally, much has been written about Germany's form of capitalism and whether the "German Model" remains viable and distinct, or converging with a liberal-market model embodied by the United States (Hall & Soskice 2001; Streeck & Thelen 2005; Dyson & Padgett 2006). Much attention is devoted to Germany's system of labour-management relations (Herrigel 2000; Silvia 2013), vocational training system (Thelen 2007), regulatory system (Dyson 1992), and financial system (Deeg 1999; Krahnen & Schmidt 2004). This research makes the case that public banks are an important part of Germany's "special sauce" that enables the country to sustain its unique type of capitalism. Germany's system of local public banks not only complements other political and economic institutions (Deeg, 2007) but has shown to be a stabilizing force upon which the entire economy depends. At the same time, Sparkassen, offers a window into (1) the domestic, European, and international forces pressuring Germany to adapt to a liberal-market model; and (2) the ways in which domestic actors and institutions defend the country's model of capitalism.

Book outline

The book has six chapters. This first introduces Germany's local public savings banks and the core questions at the centre of this book. Chapter 2 describes the Sparkassen's place within Germany's banking system, the features that define

Sparkassen within a larger public banking network, and what sets Sparkassen apart from other private and public credit institutions. The chapter devotes particular attention to the distinction between Sparkassen and other types of alternative banks including regional or federal development banks that have sprung up in recent years. Chapter 3 draws on the work of comparative political economists and banking scholars to flush out the ways in which Sparkassen are such an enigma in today's world of global finance: how Sparkassen's performance in the past twenty years defies scholarly expectations.

With a clear understanding of what public savings banks are (and are not) and the puzzles surrounding them, the subsequent three chapters present the empirical evidence supporting my answer to how Sparkassen remained so resilient in the face of global, European and domestic pressures and widespread expectations of their demise. Chapter 4 begins with the explanation that is the most proximate to banks' customers and communities. Sparkassen are resilient because of the economic strength of local economies and the economic value the credit institution provide local communities. The chapter draws on examples and quantitative data to illustrate the symbiotic relationship between a Sparkasse and the local economy: how a local economy strengthens a savings bank and how a savings bank directly and indirectly promotes a local community. Economists typically measure the value of a company in terms of financial performance or share value. However, Sparkassen stabilized regions of Germany during the financial crisis by supplying a steady flow of capital to local businesses and municipal governments when private commercial banks cut back on lending. The experience underscores the importance of Sparkassen beyond what is typically captured in a balance sheet. Because they are embedded in a community, Sparkassen are significant sources of social capital – providing support to schools, local clubs, infrastructure projects, and affordable housing. The chapter analyzes the contribution Sparkassen made (and continue to make) to Germany's economy, particularly the most vulnerable parts of the economy. At the same time, the chapter also makes clear that economic explanations are insufficient to explain the resilience of Sparkassen. Sparkassen appear to thrive even in poorer regions of the country. And economic explanations fail to explain why or how Sparkassen resisted the temptation to gamble on the US subprime housing market or how they were able to prevent policies from being adopted that challenged their business model.

Chapter 5 turns to organizations and administration as explanations for Sparkassen's resilience. Economic theory suggests that during tight fiscal times public institutions should be vulnerable to risk-taking pressures, particularly as industry leaders like the large commercial banks and Landesbanken reap significant returns. Public savings banks in other countries like Spain's *cajas* suffered losses from risky investments (Deeg & Donnelly 2016; Garicano 2012). One would expect Sparkassen to follow but they did not. In addition, one would expect small independent credit institutions like Sparkassen to struggle to compete with larger private banks, particularly as regulatory burdens rose in the aftermath of the financial crisis. The chapter argues that organizational structures and administrative factors kept Sparkassen from the risk-taking adventures that sunk Landesbanken and commercial banks, and enabled Sparkassen to successfully compete with much larger private institutions. The chapter devotes particular attention to Sparkassen's unique governing structures including an overlapping committee system that keeps politics separate from administration. The chapter also analyzes Sparkassen's multiple deposit insurance systems and joint liability scheme which increases accountability while also reinforcing Sparkassen's central position within local economies. At the same time, the chapter argues that economics and administration alone are insufficient to explain how Germany's public savings banks succeeded in preventing a number of domestic and international policies from being adopted that directly challenge their business model.

Power and politics are the focus of Chapter 6. Sparkassen's ability to prevent policies that undermine their business model is a function of their power and influence. According to *Der Spiegel*, Germany's Sparkassen are the most powerful interest group in all of Germany. Chancellor Angela Merkel has never missed speaking at the annual meeting of the DSGV, the interest group that represents Sparkassen. The public savings banks' political power shaped the architecture of Europe's banking union and has influenced local, state and national policies. The chapter defines Sparkassen's power, explores the sources of that power, and then discusses two critical cases – one at the EU level and one at the local level – where one can see Sparkassens' power in action. One case is an effort by the European Union to adopt an EU-wide banking union. A second case is Sparkassen's successful effort at limiting the amount of dividends paid to cities and counties. Both cases illustrate how Germany's public savings banks use their power to stave off global and domestic efforts to weaken them.

A final section of the book turns to the future of Germany's public savings banks and the lessons Sparkassen offer for global efforts to establish similar institutions. Chapter 7 examines efforts in other countries, particularly the United States, to establish credit institutions similar to Sparkassen.

2

CONTEXT

"We're for-profit, not profit-maximizing" – Sparkassen CEO

In her historical account of banking in the United States *The Politics of Banking* (2001), Susan Hoffmann argues that depository institutions are the product of policy choices. Hoffmann, along with work by comparative political economists and students of public banking resist the temptation to view banks as generic economic actors that arise naturally to serve the demands of markets. There is nothing natural or inevitable about credit institutions. Instead, Hoffmann and others demonstrate that credit institutions are the result of political choices over the entity's institutional features, and its mission and purpose (Hackethal *et al.* 2006; Butzbach 2008).

This chapter draws on Hoffmann's insights to introduce Germany's Sparkassen. The chapter is organized around a set of questions that offer a primer on Germany's public savings banks: Where do Sparkassen originate? What sets them apart from other credit institutions? Where do they fit within Germany's banking system and what is their business model? And finally, how are public savings banks organized and governed? The chapter begins with a historical account of the origins of Sparkassen's mission. A second section outlines the institutional features that distinguish Sparkassen from other banks. A third section discusses where Sparkassen fit within the country's network of public banking. And finally, the chapter considers where Sparkassen fit within Germany's federal banking system.

A mission forged in crisis

Studies of German industrialization often focus on the role large banks played in enabling Germany to leapfrog other advanced economies in the nineteenth and early twentieth century (Gerschenkron 1989; Shonfield 1969). Scholars attribute to Germany's large private universal banks the leading role in the development of the country's industry. However, smaller credit institutions such as cooperatives and public savings banks also played an essential role in Germany's transition from an agrarian to industrial capitalism. It is a role that continues to reverberate in today's economy perhaps even more so than the impact of big banks.

Prior to 1871, Germany was a group of independent states rather than a single country. Banking laws and related regulatory issues were left to the individual states unless specifically negotiated through treaties. Sparkassen thrived in Germany's pre-1871 fragmented system in part because of their banks' diversity. Sparkassen could be chartered as private institutions or as entities owned and controlled by any level of government including a municipality, district or a province. Guinnane (2001: 19) notes that in Prussia most savings banks were chartered by a city or a provincial government. In the larger cities, the savings banks were linked to a specific neighbourhood. In rare cases Sparkassen could belong to a firm or professional organization.

Public savings banks were also instrumental in financing government debt. Most German states were burdened with a sizeable debt in the decades prior to unification in 1871 (Tilly 1980: 61). Governments turned to Sparkassen deposits to finance their debt and navigate the economic upheavals of the nineteenth century. Savings banks were thus a source of economic and political stability in the lead up to unification. However, Sparkassen's most important contribution to Germany's economic and political development in the nineteenth century was their relationship to the poor and working classes.

Industrialization created a large class of poor and working people who were excluded from financial services at a time when those financial services were needed most. Industrialization drove peasants from rural areas – into cities. Also, as they migrated from farms to cities in search of employment and a better life, families were easy targets for exploitation by landlords and employers (Deutscher Sparkassen- und Giroverband 2010). Before the invention of savings banks, it was common for poor and proletariat classes to rely on pawn shops and other forms of private usury (Führer 2001). Also, small- and medium-sized enterprises (SMEs) were often excluded from financial services as privately-held banks catered exclusively to elites and large companies (Henneke 2019: 41). Urban migration also left the poor and working-class vulnerable to disease, homelessness and malnutrition. Sparkassen gave the poor and working classes a tool to cope with the harmful consequences of industrialization. The savings banks were part of an international movement to provide a safe place for the poor and working class to desposit their savings.[3] Ashauer (1991) notes for example that in 1850 two-thirds of Munich's Sparkassen savers were either peasants or workers. In Prussia's Sparkassen between 1850–1908 a third of all accounts held less than 60 Marks. As Hans Pohl (2005: 23) writes, Germany's Sparkassen emerged, "During the time of pauperism ... to give the poorest classes the ability to become self-reliant in the face of sickness, disability, and old-age".

Sparkassen, in other words, were established as a unique policy solution to the public problem of groups and classes being excluded from access to financial services. One can approach the problem of financial exclusion in different ways (Bresler *et al.* 2006). The state can aggressively regulate the financial industry and compel commercial banks to offer financial services to the poor and small enterprises. This establishes a right for all citizens, however, the cost of control and bureaucracy needed to enforce the regulation is considerable. A second alternative is for the state to encourage banks to adopt voluntary codes of conduct. While less costly and bureaucratic, banks might ignore the codes of conduct or pay them only lip service. A third alternative, embodied by Sparkassen and cooperatives, is for the financially excluded to organize themselves; to use the savings of the poor and proletariat to capitalize and establish a credit institution for the disenfranchised and historically marginalized groups.

German public savings banks were established in the eighteenth century by private associations (with public support) to decrease poverty and foster self-reliance through saving (Henneke 2019). One of the first savings banks established in 1778 in Hamburg extended the poorest class (*"Ersparungsklasse"*) the ability to set aside small amounts of savings to deal with unforeseen hardships (Netzel 2006). Other cities also established Sparkassen around the same time, including Kiel (1796), Göttingen (1801) and Stuttgart (1818). The next step was to place these new private credit institutions under public ownership. In 1838 Prussia passed the Prussia Savings Bank Act which placed all 234 Prussian savings banks at the time under the direct control of the respective local government for the first time. Other German states followed suit. By the beginning of the twentieth century 2,700 public savings banks were located throughout the country (Finanzgruppe Deutscher Sparkassen- und Giroverband 2010).

While they were never a solution to the exploitation, public savings banks gave the most vulnerable a place to secure their savings, earn some interest, and borrow for emergencies. Public savings banks were intended to provide the most vulnerable in society an opportunity to save for retirement or the education of their children or unforeseen crises. The new public banks also offered an alternative to exploitative usury practices that were often the only option the poor and small businesses had for credit. Cooperatives fulfilled a similar aim at a similar point in time. In 1850, the Eilenberger Vorschußverein, founded by Hermann Schulze-Delitzsch, established the first cooperative credit institution in a town. Cooperative credit institutions were founded in rural areas as *"Darlehenskassenverein"* (lending associations), based on the ideas of Friedrich Wilhelm Raiffeisen (Bresler *et al.* 2006: 248). In short, these new alternatives to private commercial banks sought to include new classes of individuals and businesses into the financial system. Sparkassen fulfilled a secondary political role as well.

Public savings banks were a paternalistic and conservative response to the exploitation and hardships of industrialization. Elites saw savings banks as instruments that enabled the masses to develop self-reliance by giving the poor and working-class access to credit, financial education, and the ability to integrate into the new capitalist economy. The view held that society's problems were not because of the new system of corporatist capitalism but the lack of self-reliance and thrift among the masses. The underlying assumption was that the poor needed to learn the importance of saving and self-discipline. Given their close democratic connection to the people, Sparkassen were the ideal institutions to teach savings and thrift. At the same time, by reducing exploitation from usury practices and giving the working poor a place to save their wages, elites also hoped to deflect support away from democratic socialists, communists, and others calling for more radical solutions to the exploitation from Germany's top-down industrial corporatism (Wehler 2006: 890). Like Bismarck's efforts at social insurance, nineteenth-century German elites believed savings banks would stabilize society during a period of immense change (van Meerhaeghe 2006).

What set savings banks apart from their predecessors was two-fold: first, in contrast to existing banks, savings banks' capital did not come from bank owners or wealthy individuals (Butzbach 2008). Instead, savings banks were capitalized with people's deposits, the third alternative to financial inclusivity that was neither strong regulation from the state nor voluntary codes of conduct. Sparkassen were capitalized with the savings of customers whom commercial banks did not serve because the sums of money were not significant enough. Second, savings banks were important sources of capital for local governments to finance infrastructure and other public goods, and, later to individuals to purchase a home or finance small businesses.

Thus, at their origin, public savings banks' mission consisted of four components: (1) to promote savings and self-reliance among the weakest in society; (2) to provide the economically weakest and most marginalized a secure place to keep their savings; (3) to provide local governments with capital needed for infrastructure; and (4) to supply local businesses and citizens with resources for housing and economic development. The core elements of their original mission remain consistent through to today.

As banks under public law Sparkassen have a public mandate (*"öffentlicher Auftrag"*) which requires that they serve their local stakeholders and local communities. Therefore, while they operate as for-profit businesses, Sparkassen do not maximize profits. Those mandates are reflected in state laws that require Sparkassen to:

- promote savings and asset building;
- ensure access to financial services to all individuals;
- promote savings and the creation of wealth (for example, by way of financial education in schools);
- maintain a presence throughout their geographical area of business (including in rural areas); and, in particular,
- safeguard the provision of loans to regional enterprises (Schackmann-Fallis *et al.* 2017).

The 2015/16 refugee crisis in Germany illustrates how Sparkassen fulfill their public mandate. In addition to contributing to refugee assistance organizations through their endowment funds, Sparkassen were required by state laws to establish bank accounts for refugees who settled in the area. Private banks and cooperatives often refused to offer refugees accounts because refugees lacked proper identification (Timmler 2016). In 2016 over a million people lived in Germany without a bank account, many of whom were refugees and asylum seekers. The *Süddeutsche Zeitung* reported, "While Sparkassen offer asylum seekers bank accounts, all other banks attempt to prevent those who have been granted legal asylum from getting an account" (quoted in Timmler 2016: 16). Deutsche Bank and Commerzbank, two of the largest private banks, were criticized by the Refugee Council of Baden Württemberg for failing to open accounts for refugees (Shotter 2016). Lack of a bank account is a significant problem for refugees, employers, and governments because Germany relies so heavily on a bank transfer system for employment and social service provisions. There is no cheque-writing system, credit card usage remains underdeveloped, and governments typically lack a cash account from which to pay out social benefits. As one Sparkasse CEO put it, "You cannot do anything in Germany without a bank account" or as a national paper put it, "It is almost impossible to survive without a bank account. If you do not have one, you cannot get a job, find housing, or receive a tax refund"[4] (Arnold 2016). In one case, Anas Albasha, a Syrian refugee who arrived in Germany in 2014 tried to open a bank account but was repeatedly rejected. After a year of trying, he was finally successful at the Sparkasse. The *Financial Times* wrote that, "German officials are keen for refugees to open bank accounts ... because transactions made through the banking system are far easier to monitor" (Shotter 2016).

Sparkassen remain the go-to banking institutions for refugees and new immigrants. In some cases, Sparkassen established special branches solely for the use of refugees and asylum seekers (Arnold 2016). Local governments, in turn, depended on Sparkassen bank accounts to distribute financial assistance (Staff 2016). The region of Hessen-Thuringia reported that between 2014 and 2016, the peak of the refugee migration, the number of special "Citizen Accounts" (so-call

"*Bürger Kontos*"), which require less documentation, jumped by 33 per cent from 133,246 to 177,026 accounts. The Berliner Sparkasse set up two specialist centres to cope with the surge in demand opening 120 accounts a day or more than 19,000 accounts by May 2016. Overall, Sparkassen opened more than 250,000 basic accounts for refugees (Schotter 2016).

In short, Sparkassen are for-profit entities with a mission established over two hundred years ago that eschews profit maximization in favour of a set of public objectives. The institutional features that define Sparkassen complement their mission.

Institutional elements

Germany's public savings banks are authorized and governed primarily by state laws ("Sparkassengesetze") in all 16 German states. While each state-law is unique, three important institutional features common to all state laws distinguish Sparkassen from other depository institutions: (1) a regional principle that formally links the bank to a specific jurisdiction; (2) a public identity which places the banks under public rather than private commercial law; and (3) a democratic system of internal governance that formerly connects citizens to banks through municipal trusteeship.

Regional principle

Public savings banks are designed to serve a specific region. Under the so-called "regional principle", state laws restrict Sparkassen from doing business outside the community in which they are located (Gärtner & Flögel 2017). A similar regional principle applies to cooperative banks as well. The principle is embedded within Article 28, Paragraph 1 of Germany's constitution which codifies constitutional protections of local self-governance.[5] The Basic Law requires that an institution of public law ("*Anstalt des öffentlichen Rechts*") founded by a municipality to provide credit to the regional economy can only be active within the territory of the municipality that establishes it. It limits public banks' business and lending to the defined administrative region in which they are headquartered. The 385 savings banks include more than 13,000 branches that link each bank to its region.

The jurisdiction of each bank is relatively small, generally no larger than one or two counties or a single large city. The rule prevents savings banks from "cherry-picking" customers from more prosperous regions of the country. A Sparkasse in one part of the country, for example, cannot offer loans or investments to potential clients of another Sparkasse. "The regional principle", according to a

Figure 2.1 The business districts of the Sparkassen and Sparkassen regional associations, 2020
Source: DSGV 2019.

DSGV executive, "means they have to stay in the region where they are. They cannot go over to the Cayman Islands or Asia. You can't earn one euro more abroad. It also means they keep the mortgages on the books. There's no securitization of loans which means the banks are responsible for credit risk. They're responsible for whatever comes up in their region."

The assumption behind the regional principle is that money saved by citizens in a locality should be used primarily to foster that localities' economic development. Consistent with their mission, the regional principle compels the public savings bank to earn their revenue by serving and investing in the local community rather than investing elsewhere. As another DSGV executive put it: "Because Sparkassen are restricted to doing business only in their region, they are forced in a sense to be engaged and active in their local economy because they don't have a choice".

As a result, the principle places an institutional brake on the growth of public savings banks, forcing them to grow slowly and deliberately. Equally important, the regional principle requires savings banks to develop local knowledge and expertise about their private and business customers in order to thrive. Moreover, because the success of an individual branch is linked to the economic success of the city or county, the regional principle incentivizes the bank to pursue the long-term economic development of the region. Their autonomy enables savings banks to adapt services that fit the needs of the particular locality. And finally, because they cannot rely on cross-subsidization from wealthier regions, savings banks are subject to often fierce market pressures (from cooperatives and private banks) to perform.

In Germany as well as throughout Europe, there is political and economic pressure to eliminate the regional principle and give savings banks the ability to do business in other parts of the country or other countries. In 2014, for example, Germany's federal Monopoly Commission released a report criticizing the Sparkassen's regional principle as anti-competitive (Mußler 2014). In its 2014 report, the Monopoly Commission wrote, "[T]he regional principle ... mainly serves to protect the savings banks against the competitive advances of the other savings banks and to fend off competition from the group as a whole" (Monopolkommission 2014: 676). Alternatively, consider the case of Spain.

The Spanish government liberalized their public savings banks known as "Cajas" in 1998, allowing them to do business outside their regions in order to give them greater opportunities to grow, expand and compete (Carles Maixé-Altés 2010). Beneficiaries of the Caja's activities including local politicians, regulators and businesses urged the savings banks to be more aggressive in their lending and to expand their market share. The hope among national politicians and regulators in Spain was that expansion and greater competition between the Cajas would lead to consolidation and modernization. Unfortunately, liberalization and deregulation led to the Cajas' spectacular downfall and ruin. Spain asked for and received a €100 billion bailout from the European Stability Mechanism in exchange for a commitment to support European banking union. The elimination of the regional principle, in particular, encouraged Cajas to invest in risky real estate schemes for which they lacked both expertise and competence, and the insurance scheme to cope with the losses (Stefan & Jorge 2018; Deeg & Donnelly 2016).

Institutions under public law

Public savings banks are not just regional, they are also independent institutions incorporated under public law.[6] The legal status means that savings banks have no "owner" nor can they be sold or privatized. This status further ensures that savings banks function as for-profit institutions with a public mission rather than as profit-maximizing firms. There is no pressure, for example, to distribute dividends to shareholders (in the case of private banks) to members (in the case of cooperatives). The public legal status is an institutional feature than enables Sparkassen to fulfill a public mandate.

Sparkassen were initially established as bureaucratic arms of local government. As noted in the previous section, the savings banks were closely intertwined with their local government sponsors who used the banks to pursue their political agendas. During the economic turmoil of the 1920s, public banks suffered from a high exposure to local government debt. Then, in 1931, the federal government loosened the tight grip of local governments by granting Sparkassen greater independence and defining them as a public law authority. The designation gave the savings banks an autonomous legal status, placed them under state savings banks laws, and subject to government supervision.

At the same time, a so-called guarantor liability (*"Gewährträgerhaftung"*) was introduced which made the municipality or county "owner" liable for depositors and third-party lenders to the bank. Additionally, local governments were also required to bear the so-called institutional liability (*"Anstaltslast"*). Institutional liability holds a municipal sponsor responsible for ensuring its savings bank can perform statutory functions and meet its financial obligations at all times. The changes made local governments accountable for the health of their institution. The maintenance obligation essentially rules out bank defaults and thus the guarantee obligation is rarely invoked. Rather than bailouts by public owners, public savings banks that struggle typically merge with healthy banks within the public banking system.

Notwithstanding their legal independence, from 1933 to 1945 municipal and county governments played an active role in steering the business practices of public savings banks. The fascist National Socialist German Workers Party (NSDAP) used public savings banks for political and military aims (Wissenschaftsförderung der Sparkassen-Finanzgruppe e.V 2011: 12). In 1933 there were over 3,000 Sparkassen in the Third Reich. And Sparkassen played a central role in the elimination of Jewish businesses and the "Aryanization" of communities (D'Acunto *et al.* 2013). And because savings banks had most of the country's retail customers, the Nazi regime relied on savings banks to promote a massive national campaign to raise the capital necessary to pay for the war effort. With the establishment of the Federal Republic of Germany in 1949, Sparkassen became again independent entities, no longer directly dependent municipal institutions.

Today, Sparkassen are completely independent entities subject to the German Banking Act, state-level public savings bank laws, and EU bank and financial markets regulations. While public savings banks were initially capitalized with local government funding, they are today capitalized exclusively with equity from bank revenues. Local governments no longer hold any equity stake in the bank. Moreover, state laws prevent municipal governments from directly intervening in a banks' business strategy. In addition, in 2001 the European Commission, the German government, and the DSGV agreed to abolish the "guarantor liability" and the "institutional liability" by July 2005.

At the same time, Sparkassen should not be confused with state banks, promotional banks or development banks. There are many development banks (*"Förderbanken"*) in Germany. Each of Germany's 16 state governments has a development bank. Moreover, the most recognized development bank at the federal level, the Kreditanstalt für Wiederaufbau ("KfW"), is the third largest bank in Germany. Created after the Second World War as part of the Marshall Plan to help redevelop the country, the KfW pursues explicitly political objectives such as subsidizing particular German companies and industries, distributing economic assistance in developing countries, and stock purchases of Germany's privatized postal service (Deutschen Post AG) and telecommunications utility (Deutschen Telekom AG).

Development banks differ from public banks both in their mission and their governance. While Sparkassen and development banks may share a goal of promoting economic growth of a region, development banks are expressly not-for-profit institutions charged with carrying out specific public policy objectives. Development banks are also direct instruments of government. The KfW, for example, is the central tool of the federal government to help companies in crisis. In pursuit of specific public objectives, such as the KfW's work distributing assistance to businesses harmed by the coronavirus, development banks are prohibited from competing with public, cooperative or private for-profit banks. Thus, while the EU in 2001 ended public guarantees of solvency for Sparkassen and Landesbanken, the European Commission allows governments to continue to guarantee the solvency of promotional banks because they do not violate rules governing competitive markets. Finally, as arms of federal and state administrations, the management of promotional banks are filled with political appointments. Such personnel practices stand in contrast to the management practices of Sparkassen which are kept separate from politics. In short, the mission and governing structure of promotional banks make them more political by design than local public savings banks.

Interestingly, from its inception the former German Democratic Republic (GDR) also adopted public savings banks as the primary source of retail banking in the country (Henneke 2019: 70; Pohl *et al.* 2005: 397–408). As in the West, East German Sparkassen were also public entities. However, unlike West Germany where the institutions were decentralized and independent, East German Sparkassen were state entities organized around dual federalism. The GDR's savings banks (like other economic sectors) were a part of the centralized state's Ministry of Finance in Berlin; branches of the State Bank (Staatsbank). At the same time, Sparkassen were also part of the East German district's (*Bezirke*) economy and thus accountable to local politicians. East German Sparkassen managers needed approval of local politicians for furniture or supplies. Local officials oversaw savings banks' finances (Wysocki & Günther 1998).

At the time of the Soviet occupation of East Germany there were 310 Sparkassen. The number of savings banks fluctuated with various administrative reforms to local government jurisdictions. In 1952 there were 198 Sparkassen in the GDR and the banks served as tools of the centrally planned economy. Their mission was limited to fostering savings, enabling cash transfers, facilitating small amounts of lending, and financing large-scale public housing construction. Notably missing from the East German savings banks was a connection to the local government or the promotion of the local economy. The omission was partly a function of the country's centrally planned system and the lack of local commercial activity (Henneke 2019: 70–72; Wysocki & Günther 1998; Finanzgruppe Deutscher Sparkassen- und Giroverband 2010).

Notwithstanding their limited role in the East German economy, Sparkassen were nevertheless a significant presence in the country. According to current managers of former East German Sparkassen, the savings banks were very much a part of East German society. The institutions employed a lot people, particularly women. By some estimates, 90 per cent of employees in GDR's Sparkassen were women. Moreover, most East Germans saved their East German marks in Sparkassen which turned out to be fortuitous after unification and currency union on 1 July 1990. Former East Germans could, per adult, exchange up to 4,000 East German marks at an exchange rate of 1 to 1.[7] Prior to the fall of the Berlin Wall, East Germans were not allowed to exchange their currency for West German currency. The East/West exchange rate was set by the East German government and fluctuated between 3 or 4 East German marks to one West German mark. In the final months of the GDR the black-market exchange jumped to one West German mark to 11 East German marks (Paulick 2010; Cassell 2002). Thus, with a stroke of a pen, the value of the deposits saved in East German Sparkassen increased significantly.

Municipal trusteeship

A final institutional feature that distinguishes Sparkassen from private banks and cooperatives is their formal connection to citizens (Henneke 2019: 255). Just as Article 28(2) of Germany's Constitution or Basic Law codifies local self-governance, Article 20(1) requires a democratic connection from the people to the decisions made by local governments. Sparkassen are included in this constitutional provision. The creation and promotion of the Sparkassen's public mission must be based ultimately on the will of the people. This democratic principle is fulfilled through a system of municipal trusteeship in which elected representatives of the locality sit on the governing body overseeing a Sparkassen.

German public savings banks have a two-tier board structure: a supervisory board (known as *"Verwaltungrat"*) and a management board (known as *"Vorstand"*). They are separated from each other and there are no personal or personnel connections between board and management. Two-thirds of the supervisory board consists of representatives from local government sponsors, and one-third of the board are representatives of bank employees. The top local official in the jurisdiction, typically a county executive (*"Landrat"*) or mayor (*"Bürgermeister"*) chairs the supervisory board.

The supervisory board meets quarterly and serves two important democratic roles. First, as representatives of the people the board selects and oversees the bank's management committee which includes the CEO. Management board appointees also require the approval of the Federal Financial Supervisory Authority (Bundestanstalt für Finanzdiesnstleistungsaufsicht or BaFin). Critics of Sparkassen often accuse supervisory boards of being overly politicized and poorly trained. Ralf Jasny, finance professor at the University of Applied Sciences in Frankfurt, stated, "It is difficult to determine the competency in the majority of Sparkassen-controlling boards. The knowledge gap is often so large that it cannot be made up in a couple of weekend seminars" (quoted in Poppe 2018). The criticism, however, is somewhat overstated. Supervisory boards are legally limited in their involvement in the daily activities of savings banks. Interviews with CEOs and supervisory board members reveal that supervisory boards play an active role in hiring the CEO and the management committee, setting management compensation, and determining general policies around, for example, expansion, contraction, and location of branch offices. At the same time, supervisory boards cannot and do not intervene in the daily operational decisions of the bank. Thus, while supervisory boards supervise management, the boards are not in a position to regulate the bank. Regulation occurs through other mechanisms discussed in later chapters. As a result, Hallerberg and Markgraf (2018: 45) note, "Despite the fact that supervisory boards of Sparkassen were dominated by elected local politicians ... politicization and insufficient qualification did not translate into poor bank management".

Second, supervisory boards fulfill the democratic principle by serving as the institutional mechanism through which a region's concerns and needs are inserted into the bank's policies and promoted. Supervisory boards ensure a direct connection between the bank and the people. According to several Sparkassen CEO's such regional needs might include a new economic development project in need of a loan, providing local firms with information about their industry, or helping refugees secure a bank account in order to receive public assistance. In addition, the supervisory board inserts the region's interests into the bank's policies through charitable work supporting local causes and civic organizations.

German public savings banks are the largest non-government contributor to civic organizations, local clubs, school projects, hospitals, cultural institutions, and other "social responsibility projects". For example, the Sparkasse Oberhessen, is a medium-size bank headquartered just north of the city of Frankfurt am Main. In 2019, the bank awarded grants to over 600 organizations including sports clubs and cultural organizations as diverse as a volunteer fire department, a history club, several football clubs, and a group that helps children with cancer.[8] The range of grants reflects not only the needs and interests of the region but illustrates how Sparkassen are able to tailor their work to the specific communities that oversee them. Moreover, the assistance affects Germany's broader political economy.

Germany has one of the highest levels of social capital among advanced industrialized countries. Social capital refers to the "collective value of all 'social networks' [who people know] and the inclinations that arise from these networks to do things for each other ['norms of reciprocity']" (Putnam 2000). Sparkassen play a significant role in ensuring that social capital is maintained and reproduced. In 2018 the S-Group contributed €448 million for a range of "social responsibility projects" that included: arts and culture (€133.7 million, or 32 per cent of total funds); social assistance projects (€112.6 million, or 27 per cent of total); environmental projects (€7.3 million, or 2 per cent of total); research and science (€21.4 million, or 5 per cent of total); and sports (€90.7 million, or 22 per cent of total).

Apart from charitable giving, addressing the needs of a region can also take the form of direct payments. State banking laws allow public savings banks to pay dividends (*"Ausschütungen"*) to local governments from the revenues the bank earns (Atzler 2016). State laws differ somewhat over how dividends can be spent and for what purposes dividend payments can be used. However, all state laws allow for dividends even though most Sparkassen resist the practice.

In one famous case, the mayor of Düsseldorf, Thomas Geisel (SPD), fought with his public savings bank, the Stadtsparkasse Düsseldorf, over a dividend pay-out (Mußler 2015a; Spiegel Online 2016). The bank earned €104 million in profits in 2014 and the bank's management board wanted the entire amount to be added to its capital. The bank's position faced significant opposition. As mayor of the bank's largest sponsoring entity, Geisel demanded some of the profits be paid-out in the form of dividends to the city and other local government sponsors. Ultimately, the bank lost, and the city succeeded in compelling Düsseldorf's Sparkasse to payout a dividend (Spiegel Online 2016).

A Bundesbank study estimates about a third of Sparkassen pay out dividends to their local government sponsors and that most Sparkassen could pay out a dividend while still maintaining adequate capital reserves (Köhler 2016). What enables Sparkassen to keep from paying out dividends is discussed in more detail in Chapter 6. Interestingly, the Bundesbank study found little relationship between the wealth of the region and the likelihood a Sparkassen would pay out a dividend. Savings banks in wealthy parts of the country like Baden-Württemberg and Bavaria rarely pay out a dividend, whereas Sparkassen in less well-off area like Saarland and former East German states often pay out dividends.

In short, Sparkassen are very much shaped by a set of institutional features that include their regional principle that limits where they can do business, their legal definition under public law, and their trustee relationship to local governments. In addition, Sparkassen are also part of a larger public banking network which also profoundly shapes how they operate. Chapter 5 explores how the network affects the Sparkassen's performance and reliance. The next section describes the network.

Sparkassen and the S-Group

Sparkassen are the foundation of an extensive network known as the Savings Banks Finance Group or "S-Group". With €2.2 trillion in assets (DSGV 2018), the S-Group would be one of the largest banks in the world if it operated as a single bank rather than as a network. For comparison, the two largest banks, Mitsubishi UFJ Financial Group and the Bank of China each hold assets of approximately US $2.6 trillion. The S-Group is an enormous network of financial entities that consist of 530 companies, 17,530 branches and 301,600 employees. What sets the S-Group apart from large conglomerates like Deutsche Bank or Chase Bank, is that the S-Group is neither hierarchical nor consolidated. Each savings bank is an independent credit institution focused on its own business and its own region. Relationships within the S-Group are voluntary and cooperative.

The S-Group is organized into three-levels that complement Germany's federalist political structure. Figure 2.2 describes the relationship between the different components. At the local level are the 385 savings banks.

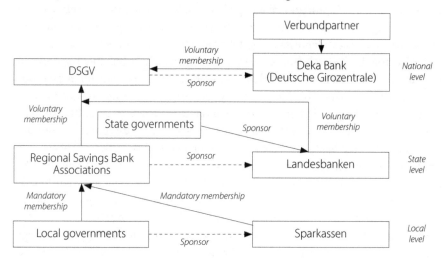

Figure 2.2 Structure of the public banking sector.
Source: cited in Brämer *et al.* (2010: 203)

As discussed in the previous section, municipal trustees or *Trägers* are mainly counties and so-called "county-free cities" (*kreisfreien Städten*) which are typically the largest cities in Germany. In 2017, 270 out of Germany's 294 counties were sponsors of 256 Sparkassen. Of the 107 county-free cities, 98 are sponsors of a Sparkasse (Henneke: 2019: 90).

At the state-level the S-Group includes six Landesbanken,[9] 12 regional savings bank associations, building and loan societies, leasing companies and insurance firms. Landesbanken are co-sponsored by a mix of state governments and regional savings associations. The mix of ownership in the Landesbanken varies from bank to bank. The Landesbank of Bavaria, for example, is owned by the Bavaria Sparkassen Association (25 per cent) and the state of Bavaria (75 per cent). The Landesbank in Saarland (SaaLB) is co-owned by the state of Saarland (74.9 per cent) and the Saarland Sparkassen Association (25.1 per cent). Others like the Landesbanken of Hessen/Thüringen and Baden-Württemberg have a more complicated mix of states, cities and Sparkassen. The ownership rights within the S-Group are weaker than the ownership rights of a private stockholder or partner of a public bank. As noted above, public bank sponsors cannot, for example, sell or privatize their local or state-level bank.

Landesbanken traditionally play three separate roles within the S-Group. First, they have access to global credit markets and provide loans to large corporations. They thus play an essential role in supporting German multinational companies. Second, Landesbanken operate as the central banks and central clearing banks for public savings banks in their region. This role ensures savings banks are integrated into supraregional and global banking. In addition, Landesbanken enable savings banks to operate more efficiently by managing their liquidity and safely investing excess deposits in capital products. In this respect, Landesbanken resemble the 11 Federal Home Loan Banks (FHLBs), government-sponsored institutions, founded in the United States in 1932. FHLB's provide financial products and services to member bank institutions in order to expand housing finance, community lending, and affordable housing (Hoffmann & Cassell 2010). And like Landesbanken, FHLBs are regional banks, sponsored by the government, and co-owned by retail banks in their region. Also, like FHLBs, Landesbanken offer financial services and products to Sparkassen (their owners) that allow them to more efficiently manage their risk. A third role of Landesbanken has traditionally been to serve as the house bank to state governments by providing public banking services to states (Gubitz 2013; Cassell 2016; Schrooten 2009).

In addition to Landesbanken, the state level also includes 12 regional savings bank associations. The regional savings bank associations are member-sponsored organizations comprising the Sparkassen and local governments in the regions. Regional associations are financed with fees levied on Landesbanken and Sparkassen. The role of the regional savings banks is two-fold. First, the associations support their members' businesses by providing economic data, legal resources, technology, and political lobbying at the state level. A second role played by the regional associations is an oversight and accountability function. Each regional association includes a *"Prüfungsstelle"*, an examining body which monitors the business practices of members and issues an annual audit of every Sparkassen in its region.

Finally, the regional level also includes eight independent regional building societies known as "Landesbausparkassen" (LBS) and 11 regional public insurance companies. The building societies are similar to savings and loan associations in that their primary purpose is to sell long-term loans (up to 30 years) at low interest rates for building housing. With a third of the building loan market, regional building societies are a major player in the country's real estate market. In 2018, the building societies made 651,000 loans worth €33 billion. The 11 regional public insurance companies known as *"Öffentliche Versicherer"* provide insurance services and products to individuals and governments in separate regions of the country. In 2018, every third German citizen had an insurance policy with the public insurance company paying €21 billion in premiums. The 11 insurance companies also control a capital investment portfolio of approximately €140 billion.

Finally, at the national level the S-Group includes the national savings bank association known as the DSGV and the Deka Bank (DekaBank Deutsche Girozentrale). The DSGV is sponsored (and financed) by the Landesbanken and the regional Sparkassen Associations. The DSGV is the umbrella organization for the S-Group and represents the interests of Sparkassen and the S-Group on banking policy and regulatory law nationally and internationally. In addition to its lobbying work, the DSGV also develops the strategic direction of the S-Group in cooperation with its numerous member parts.

The DekaBank also operates at the national level and provides the S-Group, Sparkassen, and their clients with access to the capital markets. The Dekabank is owned by the Regional Savings Bank Association. The DekaBank along with its subsidiaries (which make up the Deka Group) operate as a large investment bank, selling and managing securities and asset funds. With assets of €283 billion and 4 million managed securities accounts, the DekaGroup is one of Germany's largest securities providers. And as a member of the S-Group, the DekaBank's products are very much tailored to the risk-averse nature of its Sparkassen owners and partners.

In short, although Sparkassen are independent banks, their identity, capacity, and behaviour are very much shaped by their place within a larger public banking network. That public banking network is itself part of a large national system of banking that consists of three separate pillars.

Sparkassen and Germany's banking system

Sparkassen are part of a national banking landscape that includes universal and specialized banks (Behr & Schmidt 2016). Universal banks make up nearly 77 per cent of Germany's banking activity and combine wholesale banking, retail banking and investment banking. The Bundesbank segments universal banks further into three types or "pillars" based on their legal form and structure (see Figure 2.3).

The first pillar is private credit institutions. These institutions are privately-owned, often publicly traded, and governed under private law. The class of private banks includes the "big banks" – Deutsche Bank AG, Deutsche Postbank AG, Commerzbank AG and UniCredit Bank/Hypo Vereinsbank. There are also regional commercial banks including those who service specific industries. A third group are private banking houses with a small and limited group of owners or partners. And finally, there are subsidiaries of larger foreign banks. Private banks account for nearly 40 per cent of all banking assets in Germany of which two-thirds of total assets are produced by the "big banks" and one-third in smaller regional credit institutions and subsidiaries.

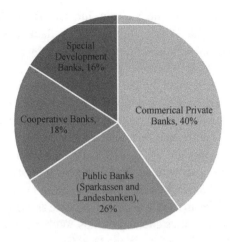

Figure 2.3 Total assets of banks in Germany (total assets in 2018 = €8,061 billion)

The second pillar consists of credit institutions under public law which hold 26 per cent of all banking assets. This pillar consists of the S-Group which includes the 385 Sparkassen and 5 Landesbanken. And finally, the third pillar comprises the cooperative banking sector, which includes approximately 900 independent institutions and one large central institution known as the DZ Bank. Cooperatives account for 18 per cent of all banking assets; most of it loans to consumers, SMEs, and farmers. While there are more cooperatives than private and public banks combined, the size of cooperatives is much smaller than the other groups. Like the S-Group, the cooperative sector consists mainly of many small local institutions and two central financial institutions. Historically, cooperative banks were seen as serving rural areas particularly in southern states, while Sparkassen served the urban working class. Over time that distinction has been eroded: the number of cooperatives has diminished significantly, they have grown in size, and they now serve a sizeable urban population. Moreover, while the number of Sparkassen branches have declined they remain a presence in nearly every county and large city in Germany.

In addition to universal banks there are specialized banks focused on specific types of banking including commercial real estate finance, savings, and home mortgage lending ("BauSparkassen"); and 16 state development banks and one national development bank, the KfW, focused on promoting economic development at the state and national levels.[10] The Deutsche Bundesbank labels these promotional banks as "banks with special tasks" (*"Banken mit Sonderaufgaben"*) and they are sometimes confused with Sparkassen or the S-Group.

Summary

Germany's local public savings banks are extraordinary for several reasons. First, their mission and institutional features, although developed over time, are clearly shaped by their origins in the early part of the nineteenth century. Sparkassen were created and designed to help those least well off overcome the struggles and exigencies of industrialization. The savings banks sought to educate the newly emerging proletariat classes about the benefits of savings and self-reliance. At the same time, the institutions were also designed to help local governments and small local businesses gain access to credit which, in turn, fostered economic growth and local democracy. Thus, while much of the literature on Germany's economic development during the nineteenth century focuses on the big banks, this brief historical overview suggests that the small savings banks also played an essential role in German political economic development.

Second, the institutional features of regionalism, public ownership and municipal trusteeship constrain the behaviour of savings banks and insert social and political values into their business model. The Oberhessische Sparkasse in the state of Hessen or the Mittelthüringen Sparkasse in the state of Thuringia are not allowed to do business outside their regions and their supervisory boards are occupied by representatives of local governments. However, these institutional features which neoclassical economics would likely view as sources of inefficiency are what enable Sparkassen to fulfill their public mission and democratic promise while still operating as a profit-seeking business. The regional principle, for example, enables local governments to service the financial needs of their constituency (a concept known in German as "*Daseinvorsorge*") in the same way that local governments are not permitted to build public pools or set up public services in other governments' jurisdictions.

A further feature that sets Sparkassen apart is that despite pressures from all sides, their business model remains "boring" (Schackmann-Fallis *et al.* 2017). For more than 200 years Sparkassen's business model has rested primarily on local deposits and local lending. They began as credit institutions capitalized with local government funds and the deposits of the working class, and they lent those deposits to individuals and small and medium-sized enterprises that had been ignored by the private banks. Today, Sparkassen are no longer capitalized with public funds nor do they enjoy any type of public guarantee, yet most lending to SMEs still originates with Sparkassen and more than 50 million German citizens has a savings account with a Sparkasse.

And finally, although they are independent, Sparkassen do not operate in isolation. Sparkassen are the foundation of a network of financial entities, political actors and societal stakeholders organized into a federalist structure but absent of hierarchy and the control. The currency within the S-Group is cooperation and decision-making from below not coercion and governance from above. The S-Group is a very large organization. Altogether its combined assets make it one of the largest financial institution in the world. However, it is a mistake to equate the S-Group with a private conglomerate or a corporation. In describing the network and the national association one executive described it:

> Sparkassen do not together form a corporation, that's important to understand. We're not a holding company and the DSGV is not the head office. We [DSGV] are an association within a broad network. We have no operational power to decide anything or require Sparkassen to do anything ... it is an extremely grassroot democratic organizational form.

Much of the attention devoted to Germany's second banking pillar focuses on the political nature of banking, on the public/private hybrid governance structures and the lack of a profit-maximizing mission. However, what distinguishes Sparkassen from other credit institutions is the way German savings banks embrace independence and connection. Sparkassen enjoy the freedom and autonomy to operate as they see fit. Yet, at the same time, their identity and institutional features link them not only to a vast network of financial entities that is the S-Group but, more importantly, grounds each public savings bank to the communities within which they operate.

3

THE PUZZLE

"In the 1990s we were criticized for being too conservative. I was the head of the Supervisory Board then and I recall the British and others saying to us that we should get rid of the Sparkassen – that they were not innovative and too conservative." – County executive and supervisory board member

With a firm grounding in the background and history of Germany's public savings banks, this chapter turns to the central puzzle of the book: What makes Germany's Sparkassen such an anomaly in the world of public savings banks? In other European countries as well as the United States local savings banks were either transformed, privatized, eliminated or consolidated to the point that they were no longer recognizable. This chapter presents the case for why Germany's Sparkassen' existence and performance are surprising; why their resilience is a puzzle worth researching.

The first section discusses how during the pre-crisis period academics and practitioners predicted and, in many cases, advocated for the weakening of Germany's bank-based model of financing. This included the elimination of what were portrayed to be antiquated and obsolete public savings banks. The epigraph by a supervisory board member at the beginning of the chapter captures the sentiment. A second section discusses the external and domestic challenges faced by Sparkassen in the aftermath of the financial crisis. Drawing on banking and economic literature, the section argues that by most accounts Germany's Sparkassen should be an endangered species. A third section of the chapter turns to their performance since the financial crisis to illustrate how Sparkassen defy expectations: that despite expectations to the contrary Sparkassen remain the most profitable and the most efficient financial institutions in Germany.

Pre-financial crisis consensus: Sparkassen are past their prime

In 2004, three years before the financial crisis hit, Manfred Weber, director of
the Association of German Banks – the largest trade group for Germany's 2,500
credit institutions – pleaded for the privatization of Germany's public savings
banks, "Local governments' bank accounts are empty as they face large deficits.
City and county officials are right to ask whether they should sell their savings
bank and invest the funds more prudently" ("Konsolidierung: 1000 Banken
werden sterben" 2004). Weber went on to predict the great consolidation of
Germany's banking sector including the death of at least a thousand banks mostly
public savings banks and cooperatives. Weber captured the consensus of the
time: Germany was overbanked. To compete globally the country needed to privatize, consolidate and eliminate the least efficient and least competitive depository institutions: public savings banks. It was a view that had culminated over
time.

Less than a decade before Manfred Weber's plea the scholar, Richard Deeg,
predicted the bifurcation of Germany's financial system. Large public and private banks would adapt to an Anglo-Saxon model of financialization because
Germany's large firms were turning to international capital markets rather than
domestic bank lending. As a result "the traditionally close relationship between
banks and large firms has loosened significantly" (Deeg 1999: 17). For Deeg and
others, the shift was more than just a blow to domestic banking institutions; it
threatened Germany's model of capitalism because it weakened banks' ability to
intervene and coordinate across firms and industries, "the relationship between
banks and large firms has developed in a manner that deviates most from the
logic of the bank-based system" (*ibid.*). Deeg also added a caveat by suggesting
that while Germany's bank-based model was likely to erode for the big banks, the
relationship between small firms and smaller banks would continue to reinforce
the bank-based model of capitalism. Deeg is one of the few scholars who deline-
ated small from large banks.

Other scholars predicted the convergence of Germany's financial system
around an Anglo-Saxon model of finance based on capital markets (Murinde *et
al.* 2004; Biswas & Löchel 2001; Lütz 2003; Grahl & Teague 2004; Albert 1993).
There was a general consensus in the early 2000s that Germany's bank-based system of capitalism was under assault from powerful domestic and international
forces: an increase in price and product competition among financial firms; technology that gave firms access to global capital markets; extraordinary growth in
new and complicated financial products; the ascendance of large multinational
corporations; and, the global integration of financial services. Taken together
these forces meant Germany's bank-based model of capitalism, embodied by the
country's public savings banks, needed to adapt to succeed or face extinction. As

evidence, scholars pointed to the demise of similar institutions in other advanced industrialized countries.

Throughout the twentieth century local public credit institutions were a pillar of national banking systems (alongside private banks and cooperatives) in most advanced industrialized countries including every country in Europe. Yet, by the start of the twenty-first century, banking industry deregulation and privatization had either eliminated most public savings banks or transformed them; removing any meaningful difference between public savings banks and conventional national and international commercial banks (Bülbul *et al.* 2013; Butzbach 2008; Ayadi *et al.* 2010). In Italy, the privatization of savings banks begins in 1990 with the Amato law, which restructured state-owned banks into joint-stock companies and changed ownership rights (Siclari 2015). The 1993 Consolidated Law on Banking furthers erodes savings banks by allowing for the consolidation of savings banks into new corporate forms (Semenyshyn 2017; Ayadi *et al.* 2009: 157–8). In France in the 1990s consolidation through mergers and acquisitions shrinks the number of savings banks from 450 small institutions to around 40 large institutions within a few years (Butzbach 2008: 149). And in Spain the financial crisis triggered a massive restructuring of the banking system leading to consolidation and a reduction in the number of savings banks from 45 to 17 (Ordóñez 2011: 26).

A similar phenomenon occurred in the United States. Banking deregulation in the 1980s transformed Savings and Loans (S&Ls) from credit institutions charged with a public mission to foster home ownership into profit-maximizing corporations that looked and behaved like commercial banks (Hoffmann 2001). Sparkassen are often compared to S&Ls (Gjelten 2008). S&Ls' transformation triggered by deregulation contributed to the S&L crisis in the late 1980s (Cassell 2002). Deregulation contributed to the loss of small community banks, particularly in rural parts of the country. Between 2008 and 2015 one in four local banks or 1,971 local credit institutions vanished in the US. Small community credit institutions – banks, S&Ls and credit unions – have become an endangered species even as federal agencies like the Federal Home Loan Bank System attempted to slow their demise (Hoffmann & Cassell 2010; Wilmarth Jr 2015). Comparative political economists' view of globalization and financialization led to a simple and straightforward conclusion: Germany's credit institutions need to grow internationally, focus on investment banking and financial services over traditional firm lending, privatize some of its public banking sector, and de-emphasize direct bank intervention in firm management in favour of more arms-length market relationships. In other words, Sparkassen had outgrown their usefulness and competitiveness. The European Union ("EU") promoted a similar view (Semenyshyn 2017).

The future of credit and finance in Europe, according to the EU, rested in the establishment of large commercial banks that could compete with the Lehman Brothers of the world and be easier to regulate than the thousands of small and diverse local credit institutions. The EU sought to expand securities markets, restrict bank holdings in non-financial firms and promote greater competition within and across member states. For the EU, Germany's fragmented public banking sector with its regional state banks and hundreds of independent public local savings banks were relics of the past not the future of European finance.

Particularly upsetting to the EU and private bankers was Germany's explicit state-backing of public savings banks and the regional Landesbanken. As noted in Chapter 2, the guarantees enabled Landesbanken to borrow on international markets at interest rates reflecting the credit ratings of the public trustees/owners rather than the banks themselves. Germany's private banks filed a complaint with the Commission in 1998 and, to the surprise of many, the Commission ruled the guarantees violated EU policy against state aid. In 2001 the EU reached an agreement with the German government and the DSGV to abolish the explicit government guarantees of public banks by July 2005. Without state guarantees Germany's public banking sector including the public savings banks were expected to contract and consolidate, behave more like private banks, and perhaps even disappear as they had throughout Europe.

To the surprise of policy analysts, politicians and experts, the changes Deeg and others predicted would happen did occur but the results did not go quite as the scholars and policy practitioners expected. First, Germany's commercial banks increased their investment banking and securitization activities, expanded their reach around the globe particularly in China, and decreased their traditional role as house banks to larger companies. Landesbanken, the regional public banks, like WestLB, BayernLB, and SachsenLB also grew in size and moved away from their traditional bank-based lending and instead road the wave of financialization (Gubitz 2013; Cassell 2016). Landesbanken expanded into new types of financial products and services, purchased the opaque subprime mortgage-backed securities and derivatives, and shifted their business model toward commission and fees and away from deposits and lending. In other words, Germany's banking system moved toward an Anglo-Saxon model just as scholars predicted and, in fact, recommended. Yet, contrary to expectations, the German banks that behaved the most like their Anglo-Saxon competitors – commercial banks and Landesbanken – performed the worst during the financial crisis and cost German taxpayers €70 billion (Deeg & Donnelly 2016; Cassell 2016). Reminiscent of the experience of S&Ls in the US during the late 1980s, the primary culprits in Germany's financial debacle were Germany's Landesbanken, Dresdner Bank, and Hypo Real Estate which fully embraced the Anglo-Saxon model (Cassell 2015).

The regional public banks comprised only approximately 21 per cent of all German banking assets prior to the crisis yet account for 41 per cent of the losses (Bofinger *et al.* 2008; see Müller 2011). Credit institutions that did not deviate from the traditional banked-based system of German capitalism, namely public savings banks and cooperatives, did surprisingly well during the crisis. Neither public savings banks nor cooperatives suffered significant losses during the financial crisis (Dietrich & Vollmer 2012; Schackmann-Fallis *et al.* 2017). As Christoph Scherrer (2014: 145) notes, "Sparkassen did well during financial crisis, in contrast to private banks and *Landesbanken*, by expanding their credit portfolio. This had a counter-cyclical impact during the crisis." Scherrer makes the important point that at the height of the financial crisis in Germany, it was local savings banks that kept the country's economy afloat. And it was precisely because Sparkassen did not choose to adopt the Anglo-Saxon method that the savings banks were able to increase credit to companies and individuals at the very moment private institutions contracted their lending. Between 2006 and 2009, new loans made by Sparkassen to businesses increased 46 per cent from €42.5 billion to €62.1 billion. Even during the worst period of the financial crisis in 2007/08 when many banks curtailed their lending, Sparkassen continued to lend to start-up firms; providing loans to an average of 7,000 new start-ups each year between 2006 and 2009 (Beck *et al.* 2009). A Bundesbank study found Sparkassen were particularly important in stabilizing the economy because German banks with the greatest exposure to the US real estate markets made their biggest cuts in lending to Germany's most fragile regions and industries, particularly those in the eastern part of the country (Ongena *et al.* 2018).

Figure 3.1 shows Sparkassen: 1) provided the largest share of lending to SMEs before and after the crisis; 2) that lending to SMEs by the large private banks and Landesbank decline significantly after the crisis, particularly the European debt crisis; and 3) lending by Sparkassen (and to a much lesser degree cooperatives) made up for the declines by big private banks and Landesbanken and kept the country in credit when it was most needed.

Domestic and international pressures since the financial crisis

Quite apart from the expectations of an Anglo-Saxon convergence in German banking, since the 2007/08 financial crisis and the European debt crisis in 2009/10 a set of domestic and international events damaged banking systems across Europe (Cassell & Hutcheson 2019). The events created new challenges for credit institutions but they imposed (and continue to impose) particular burdens on Sparkassen.

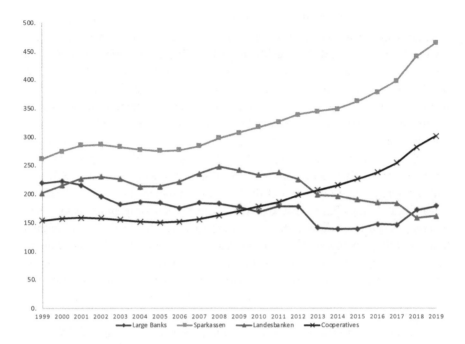

Figure 3.1 Credit provided to businesses and self-employed by banking group (in € billions)
Note: in Q2 2013, Eurex Clearing was reclassified from the non-bank sector to the credit institute sector. This affected mostly the large banks and partially explains the contraction in the volume of credit in Q2–Q3 2013.
Source: Bundesbank, LBBW Research.

Low interest rate environment

One recent challenge has been the low interest rate environment (Alessandri & Nelson 2015; Borio *et al.* 2015; Choulet 2016; Deutsche Bundesbank 2018). In the aftermath of the financial crisis the European Central Bank (ECB) launched a decade-long effort to stimulate Europe's economy to keep member states out of a recession. In 2008 the ECB allowed commercial banks to borrow money from the central bank at zero interest, but they had to promise to lend the money to businesses or consumers. More than a decade later, Europe's interest rates are -0.5 per cent, meaning it *costs* money to save with the ECB.

Low interest rates are hard on all banks because it reduces the amount credit institutions can charge for a loan and it makes savings and deposits unattractive (Braunberger 2017). However, low rates are particularly hard on Germany's public savings banks because their business model is primarily lending and deposits (Noonan 2017; Schackmann-Fallis *et al.* 2017). In 2017 the Bundesbank reported that public savings banks and other smaller credit institutions in Germany expected their "return on capital would contract by around 40 per cent if interest rates remain stable up until 2021" (Deutsche Bundesbank 2017). Reint E. Gropp, president of the Institute for Economic Research in Halle (IWH) also predicted the interest rate pressure would spell doom for Sparkassen. Gropp predicted that by 2018 public savings banks and cooperative would face a costly reckoning. And he attributed it partly to the low interest rate environment. Although a low interest environment is a problem for all banks, he stated, it is especially a problem for those that do not have other areas of business like asset management or investment banking. The big institutes are more capable of absorbing the losses than the smaller Sparkassen or cooperatives (Milde 2016).

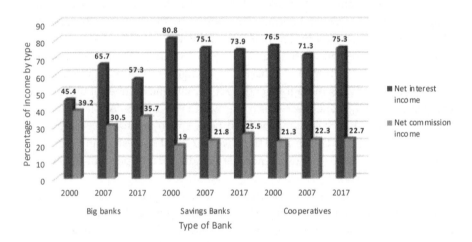

Figure 3.2 Sources of income for German banks, 2000–17
Source: Deutsche Bundesbank (2000–18).

Figure 3.2 shows the balance over time between interest income and income from commissions by banking type. Interest income is the net interest banks earn from their lending and deposits. Commission income derives from fees charged for services particularly financial services. Figure 3.2 underscores first the differences in the business model between private banks on the one hand, and savings banks and cooperatives on the other. Public banks and cooperatives depend far more on interest income than private banks. In 2000, for example, big private banks earned nearly 40 per cent of their income from commissions while savings banks earned less than 20 per cent from commissions. Private banks, by contrast, relied significantly more on commission income than savings banks. The figure also shows the impact of the low interest rate environment: between 2000 and

2017 the percentage of savings banks' income from interest has declined, from 80.8 per cent in 2000 to 73.9 per cent in 2017. At the same time, commission fees as a share of total income increased for savings banks from 19 per cent in 2000 to 25.5 per cent in 2017. The change in the balance of interest vs commission income reflects the decline in the interest rates customers are charged for borrowing.

Digitalization

A further challenge to banks generally and Germany's public savings banks in particular is digitalization or the shift to online banking (Jonietz *et al.* 2018; Deutsche Bundesbank 2018). Bank customers spend less time in bank branches and, instead, bank over the internet. As reported by the Deutsche Bundesbank (2018: 33): "Customers, who are now accustomed to using bank services and products anywhere and anytime as a matter of course, are also increasingly changing their expectations and behavior, using digital platforms to access traditional financial services more frequently". As a result, the number of technology companies offering financial services has grown in importance. At the same time the number of banks, bank branches and bank employees has fallen dramatically. The ECB reports that in 2014 there were 160,000 domestic bank branches in Europe. At the close of 2018 the number had dropped 16 per cent to 135,000 (Spiegel Online 2019).

Digitalization is a particular challenge to public savings banks because of their dense network of branches, large number of employees, and a business model built on a strong local connection between banks, SMEs and individuals in the community (Schmalzl & Wiegand 2019; Mußler 2015). A 2016 report on the future of German banking by McKinsey & Company predicted that digitalization would cause German banks to lose between 5 and 15 per cent of their interest and fee income and that, "Banks that have a high share of simple and therefore attackable products on their balance sheets (including simple retail savings and lending products) will be most affected – such as the average Sparkasse, local cooperative banks, foreign private banks, or Bausparkassen" (Koch *et al.* 2016: 6)

EU pressure and policies

Efforts by the EU and ECB to reshape the banking landscape created additional challenges for Germany's public savings banks (Semenyshyn 2017). EU policymakers have made no secret they would like European commercial banks to merge and grow in size, and for Germany's state and local public banks to privatize and disappear. In 2016, ECB President Mario Draghi made clear in a speech to the European Systemic Risk Board (which he chaired) that the biggest financial problem in Europe is that it is overbanked, "Over-capacity in some national banking sectors, and the ensuing intensity of competition, exacerbates this squeeze on margins" (quoted in Buell 2016). Put simply: there is just too much competition from the thousands of smaller banks that are crowding out the profits for the big banks. Draghi's solution is greater concentration and consolidation of the banking sector coupled with the privatization of thousands of smaller local public banks (Buell 2016). For EU policymakers, a small number of large private banks has important advantages including: 1) a reduction in intra-European competition; 2) an increase in the ability of European banks to compete with large investment banks in the US and China; and 3) a reduction in the regulatory burden for the ECB by reducing the total number and type of banks being overseen.

The EU along with the ECB pursue these goals through a variety of policies including: the ending of state guarantees of public banks; efforts to establish a European banking union consisting of a single supervisory, a single resolution mechanism, and a single European deposit insurance system; the deregulation of the loan repurchasing agreement market ("repo market"); the promotion of European-wide securitization; the effort to establish a "capital-markets union" and the opposition to financial transaction tax (Braun 2018). While designed to support large commercial banks, the EU policies pose particular challenges to Germany's public savings banks. As noted above, the end of state guarantees was meant to increase borrowing costs to local and regional public banks. The EU's banking union proposals, which initially did not exempt smaller institutions, placed a disproportionately heavier regulatory burden on smaller institutions. In response to Germany's opposition to the initial proposal, the final architecture of EU banking union limited supervision and resolution only to Europe's largest and most significant institutions leaving out Germany's local saving banks. European deposit insurance was eliminated but is likely to be reintroduced.

As discussed in Chapter 6, the European Deposit Insurance Scheme (EDIS) poses a direct threat to the public savings banks' approach (and comparative advantage) to deposit insurance. Rather than pay into a deposit insurance fund based on their risk Germany's public savings banks protect institutions and depositors through an International Protection Scheme (IPS). The EU defines an IPS as "a contractual or statutory liability arrangement which protects those institutions and in particular ensures their liquidity and solvency to avoid bankruptcy where necessary" (Article 113, Paragraph 7 CRR).[11] The entire S-Group including the public savings banks and Landesbanken are part of an IPS. This means all the parts of the S-Group share joint liability for all the other institutions and their customers. The EU's EDIS plan, modelled on the Federal Deposit

Insurance Corporation, force Sparkassen to contribute to two schemes (EDIS and IPS), undermines their competitive advantage, and threatens their existence (Semenyshyn 2017; Gros & Schoenmaker 2013). And finally, expansion of securitization, deregulation and a new capital-market union are supranational efforts to foster a market-based financial system that favours commercial banks at the expense of local public savings banks. A related challenge to EU pressure confronted by public savings banks is increased regulatory burden.

Regulatory burdens

In the wake of the financial crisis banking regulators in Europe and the United States increased the regulatory burden for all credit institutions. In Europe the three European financial supervisory authorities[12] imposed greater disclosure requirements, new capital requirements, and the adoption of a single rule book to cover all banks in Europe. The DSGV estimates that since the financial crisis supervisory authorities issued more than 180 new guidelines and 300 new technical standards with which all credit institutions, regardless of size, must comply (Engelhard 2018). The single rule book is meant to ensure the uniform application of Basel III requirements across all member states and thus close any regulatory loopholes (European Commission 2013). National banking supervisors have also increased their regulatory oversight.

The new regulations increase the demands and cost of regulatory compliance for all credit institutions. However, the regulatory burden falls disproportionately on smaller European banks like Germany's Sparkassen and cooperatives for two reasons. First, regulatory compliance is a fixed cost and larger institutions enjoy economies of scale that comes from their size; they are able to spread the cost of compliance across a much larger organization. And second, in contrast to the United States, European banking supervisors apply the same standards and regulatory burden (Basel I to III) across all banks regardless of their size and complexity. Sparkassen are credit institutions within the meaning of Section 1(1) German Banking Act ("Kreditwesengesetz [KWG]") as well as Article 4(1) European CRR. Hence, they are subject to all German and European bank regulation requirements, and to supervision by Deutsche Bundesbank and German Federal Financial Supervisory Authority ("Bundesanstalt für Finanzdienstleistungsaufsicht [BaFin]"), and/or the EECB. The United States, by contrast, differentiates between Wall Street and main street banks. The US regulators and supervisor work with small banks to reduce their regulatory burden, and while smaller US banks still complain about their regulatory burden, international standards are only applied to the large commercial banks. While large commercial banks in Europe support the single rule book (because it advantages them), small institutions like Sparkassen and cooperatives argue European banking regulation directly hurt SMEs. George Fahrenschon, former head of the DSGV, stated, "If regulators fail to recognize the importance of proportionality and maintain a one-size-fits-all system, we ... will create a new problem of 'too small to succeed'" (quoted in Moore 2017).

Landesbanken legacy

A final challenge for Sparkassen has been (and continues to be) their connection to the regional public banks, Germany's Landesbanken. Landesbanken are part of the larger S-Group network. And as already noted, Landesbanken accounted for much of Germany's losses during the financial crisis and in some cases still carry a significant number of non-performing loans on their books (Storbeck 2018). Several Landesbanken including WestLB and SachsenLB, were resolved and several others were taken over by healthier Landesbanken. There are currently six Landesbanken, down from eight before the financial crisis.

Benjamin Gubitz (2013) has written the most extensive scholarly account of Landesbanken' failure during the crisis and their connection to Sparkassen. According to Gubitz, Sparkassen's relationship with Landesbanken is complex and multi-dimensional (Gubitz 2013). First, Landesbanken are clients of Sparkassen. The regional banks provide Sparkassen with a source of liquidity and capital, a place to park their excess reserves, and a source of dividends. Landesbanken also provide Sparkassen with the capacity to provide customers with more complex financial products. In this sense, Sparkassen are clients of the Landesbanken. At the same time Sparkassen are co-owners of Landesbanken along with state governments. As co-owners Sparkassen representatives sit on the supervisory boards, the controlling bodies of Landesbanken. And finally, in recent years, Landesbanken and Sparkassen have become fierce competitors particularly in the wake of the EU's decision to end state guarantees. The combination of all three Sparkassen identities – customer, owner, and competitor – not only exposed local public savings banks to losses incurred by their larger regional banking partners but threatened (and continues to threaten) savings banks' public image as a safe and conservative credit institution (Welp 2011; Coppola 2017). In the aftermath of the financial crisis, articles in leading economic and financial publications predicted that Landesbanken would soon bring Sparkassen down with them. One article published in 2009 in the news magazine *Focus* captured the theme. The article's rhetorical title "How Healthy is the Sparkassen World?" called into question the health of Germany's savings banks and suggested their connection to Landesbanken might bring them down (Dönch *et al.* 2009).

Sparkassen defy expectations

By nearly all accounts Germany's public savings banks should be a footnote in the financial history books: either extinct or transformed into entities that resemble private commercial banks as in most other European countries. Twenty years ago scholars predicted Germany's financial system would converge on an Anglo-Saxon model of banking. Sparkassen are the antithesis of the Anglo-Saxon banking model. In addition, there is a common belief in the mainstream economics profession reflected in a robust literature on public banking globally that public banks are less profitable, less efficient, and more prone to corruption than their private competitors (see, especially, La Porta *et al.* 2002). And if convergence theories were not enough, the financial crisis coupled with multiple domestic and international forces should have nailed the coffin shut on Sparkassen. Yet, the predictions were off.

Today, it is big private banks like Deutsche Bank that struggle even as profitability among public savings banks with their "boring" business model remains stable (Ewing 2019). Germany's public savings banks largely resisted the temptation to bite at the Anglo-Saxon apple of financialization. Sparkassen largely eschewed the toxic and risky investments that sent the global economy into a tailspin (Gjelten 2008). Deeg and Donnely write that Sparkassen came through the financial crisis unscathed (Deeg & Donnelly 2016: 2). In fact, Moody's credit analysis reported in 2011 that, "[German] savings banks, emerged from the financial crisis stronger than before reporting a very solid pre-provision income of €11.8 billion (+9.3 per cent year-on-year) and a pre-tax profit of €4.6 billion (+21.6 per cent) in preliminary results".

The credit rating agency underscores Sparkassen's profitability and lending following the financial crisis. But, how have Sparkassen fared over time? How have public savings banks' profits compared with other pillars of Germany's banking system? How efficient are public savings banks compared to other institutions? And finally, at a time of low interest rates and greater competition, how has public savings banks' core business model – lending and deposits – changed? Drawing on several sources of data, we consider two indicators of resilience: profitability and efficiency.

Profitability

The domestic and external pressures confronted by Germany's credit institutions should be squeezing Sparkassen's profitability. Moreover, given the constraints on Sparkassen's ability to do business outside their regions, their public ownership structure, and the absence of a profit-maximizing mission, one should expect Sparkassen's profitability to be significantly less than their private-sector counterparts. Yet, in looking at three different measures of profitability, the data from the Bundesbank paint a different picture.

One important measure of performance for all banks but particularly public savings banks is the amount of deposits customers keep in their bank. As noted above, deposits are particularly important to Sparkassen because their primary source of revenue is their net interest income they charge to borrowers and pay to depositors. By most accounts record low interest rates and greater competition for customer savings should squeeze the profitability of Sparkassen. Both factors should trigger disintermediation, Sparkassen customers fleeing to private domestic or international banks with lower fees or who pay higher interest rates. Greater global competition and lower interest rates leads one to expect Sparkassen's deposits to decline over time. What do we see? What has happened to public savings banks during the past decade as the ECB has sought to use monetary policy to stimulate Europe's economy?

One response by all banks including Sparkassen has been a greater reliance on commissions and fees to offset the loss in interest income. As noted above, the share of Sparkassen profits from interest incomes has declined and the share from commissions and fees has increased slightly. However, what is striking is that Sparkassen deposits *increased* since the financial crisis, from €717 billion in 2007 to nearly €1 trillion in 2019, an increase of nearly 40 per cent. And the number of bank accounts has remained steady even as competition among banks has grown and the ECB has sought to stimulate the economy by keeping interest rates at record low levels.

A second common measure of a banks' success is its after-tax profit margin. The after-tax profit margin is the revenue remaining after all the operating expenses, taxes and dividends are deducted. After-tax profit margin is significant because it is not only an indicator of a company's revenue but also how well a company controls its costs. A high after-tax profit margin can mean high revenues but it also can indicate that a company runs efficiently. Figure 3.3 reports the after-tax profits as a percentage of total operating income across the three pillars of Germany's banking system from 2000 to 2018, a stretch of time that spans the period prior, during and after the financial crisis. Thus, in 2017 public savings banks' aggregate after-tax profit was 23 per cent of operating income. For the four big private banks' aggregate after-tax profits were 9.8 per cent of operating income.

The data illustrate that since the financial crisis in 2007/08 savings banks' after-tax profit margins are higher than most German banks and significantly higher than the four private banks. Second, in 2011 at the height of the European debt crisis savings banks' after-tax profit margin spiked even as profitability among the private banks caved. Third, savings bank's profitability prior to the financial crisis was also quite strong in comparison to other banks. In fact, private

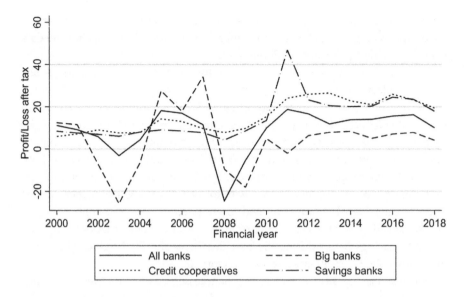

Figure 3.3 Profit/loss by bank type, 2000–18
Source: Deutsche Bundesbank (2000–18).

banks were more profitable than savings banks in only four out of the last 18 years. Finally, what is striking about the after-tax profit margin of savings banks is how stable profits are over the 18-year period. Savings banks' after-tax profit margins rose over time but, with the exception of 2011, the growth is incremental and gradual. Profitability among the big four private institutions swings dramatically over time, from the negative 20s in the early 2000s to the high 30s in the mid 2000s and then falling again to 10 from 2012 onward.

Another measure of profitability is the rate of return on equity (ROE). ROE is a key measure of performance that investors typically use to calculate the amount of a company's income that could be returned as shareholders' equity. ROE reveals how effectively a company generates profits from the equity in the business. The Bundesbank compares across pillars by reporting the ratio of profit for the financial year before tax to balance sheet capital (total equity). Figure 3.4 reports on the ROE for all three pillars from 2000 to 2018.

Bundesbank data reveal several findings that defy expectations. First, public savings banks' ROE has been higher than the average banks' ROE for nearly the entire period with the exception of the period leading up to the financial crisis, where the ROE of the four large private banks soared. A second surprise finding is that in the period during and after the financial crisis the savings banks' ROE rose dramatically and then tapered off to a level slightly higher than the period prior to the financial crisis. Moreover, savings banks' profit jumped after the

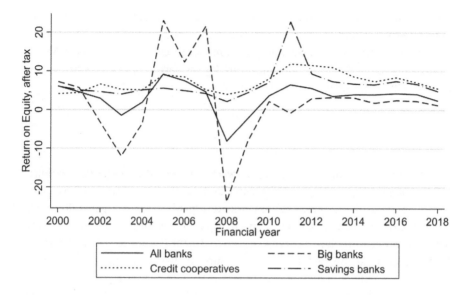

Figure 3.4 Return on equity by bank type, 2000–18
Source: Deutsche Bundesbank (2000–18).

financial crisis and declined. Yet, their ROE remained significantly higher than the ROE of the four big commercial banks and all banks generally. And finally, what stands out from the Bundesbank data is the stability of the Sparkassen's ROE compared to private banks. As with after-tax profit margins, the ROE of private banks swings wildly from +20 to –20 within a single year. By contrast, the ROE of savings banks remains positive and consistent with the exception in 2011 when Sparkassen stepped up to provide credit in the postcrisis period. In its September 2018 monthly performance report of Germany's credit institutions, the Bundesbank wrote: "Savings banks and credit co-operatives remained the most profitable categories of banks, with returns on equity of 9.4 per cent and 10.1 per cent, respectively" (Bundesbank 2018).

In short, by common measures of profitability and financial performance Sparkassen defy expectations. Assets and deposits have increased steadily since the financial crisis including during the more recent period of low interest rates. After-tax profits are consistently higher than the big private commercial banks and returns-on-equity are also higher than the big four private commercial banks. Equally noteworthy is the consistency of the Sparkassen's performance. As private banks' profitability soars and plummets, Sparkassen's "boring" business model generates far less volatility. Incremental and steady increases in Sparkassen profitability reflects the long-term, patient time horizon of their primary SME customers and individuals. At the same time, as Richard Deeg noted in 1999, the breadth and depth of the Sparkassen's presence throughout the country (in nearly every city and county) creates a powerful counterweight to global economic forces pressuring firms and governments to climb on the Anglo-Saxon bandwagon. But what about efficiency? Sparkassen earn profits and revenues but are they efficient, particularly compared with commercial banks?

Efficiency

It is common to compare efficiency between public and private organizations. Public choice scholars in political science and public administration have published libraries on the premise that private organizations are generally more efficient than public organizations, and that politicians must look to the private sector in order to replace or "reinvent" government (Osborne & Gaebler 1992; Kettl 2018). While the models used to measure efficiency are sometimes complicated, the underlying theoretical argument is straight-forward: public organizations are less efficient because politicians and public-sector employees use public organizations to pursue their personal goals (electoral advantage, higher salaries, larger budgets, more authority) rather than the public interest (Niskanen 1971; Tullock 1987; Friedman 1993). In the case of public banks, scholars contend that when governments control a community's financial leavers, politicians or bureaucrats use (or more likely abuse) their influence over credit institutions to gain votes, bribe other office holders, and loosen budget constraints (Hallerberg & Markgraf 2018; Köhler 2016; La Porta *et al.* 2002; Shleifer & Vishny 1994).

A large body of scholarship takes issue with public choice assumptions about the behaviour and motivation of politicians and bureaucrats (Amy 2011; Madrick 2009). Politicians and civil servants are asked to solve society's most difficult problems argues James Q. Wilson (2000). And the public sector has shown to be remarkably effective in tackling everything from public health to air pollution to public safety to education to innovations in technology. At the same time, scholars point to the theoretical limitations of privatization (Moe 1987; Donahue 1999; Bozeman, 2002). Empirical studies find that when we rely on private entities to deliver public goods the outcome is not efficiency but often corruption, opacity, inefficiency and higher costs (Gormley 1991; Feigenbaum & Henig 1994; Moe 1987; Suleiman & Waterbury 2019; Henig *et al.* 1988). This chapter refrains from weighing in on the debate over privatization. However, the debates inform the expectations of what administrative efficiency looks like within the three pillars of Germany's banking system.

If proponents of privatization are correct, one would expect the administrative costs of Germany's public savings banks (and cooperative banks) to be significantly higher than those in private commercial banks. Moreover, pressures to converge on an Anglo-Saxon model of banking, increased regulatory burdens, and greater global competition would lead one to expect the pillar with the largest banks to benefit from economies of scale and the comparative advantage that comes with size and global reach. Alternatively, one would expect the administrative efficiency of 385 independent public savings banks (with 385 CEOs, 385 management boards, and 385 supervisory boards) to be much lower than the efficiency of the large private publics.

Several approaches are used to gauge efficiency. The first compares the administrative costs and expenses of all three banking pillars as a percentage of operative income. Bank expenses consist of administrative spending and staff costs including wages and salaries, and contributions to pensions. Other bank expenses include each banks' contribution to an EU-mandated resolution fund, payments to maintain a network of branches, and expenses for external contracted services such as legal, auditing, and IT services.

Figures 3.5 and 3.6 report the administrative costs as a percentage of operating income and gross revenues, respectively. The cost/income and cost/revenue ratios provide standard measures of cost-efficiency used by the Bundesbank. The higher the ratio, the less operating income or revenues remain after deducting for administrative spending. The lower the ratio the more income and revenues are left over after deducting for spending. So what do the data reveal?

First, both measures of efficiency reveal private banks are significantly *less* efficient than public banks or cooperatives during the 18-year period that overlaps the financial crisis. In the early 2000s the big four banks' cost/income ratio was routinely over 90 per cent and that level of efficiency largely remained constant. As the Bundesbank reported in 2017, "Although the big banks are likely to benefit from economies of scale, they have been the banks with the highest and thus worst cost/income ratio for years" (Bundesbank 2017: 45). A second finding is that savings banks' level of efficiency is often the highest among the three pillars. In the lead up to the financial crisis, the public savings banks' cost/income ratio hovered at around 70 per cent before dropping even further during the financial crisis. Also striking is the fact that public savings banks' efficiency improved over time. The cost/income ratio in 2017 was slightly lower than in 2000 and significantly lower than in 2008.

The consistency and the improvement in the Sparkassen's efficiency over time is also reflected in data from the DSGV that tracks changes in the number of employees, branches, and the ratio of employees to assets or employees (see Table 3.1).

Between 2007 and 2018 Sparkassen became significantly leaner. The total number of Sparkassen declined by 13 per cent mostly through mergers. Sparkassen cut the number of branches by 18 per cent and in many cases replaced physical branch offices with ATM machines or even in some cases, mobile "branch"

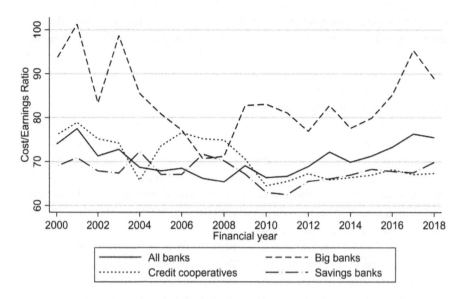

Figure 3.5 Cost/income ratio by bank type, 2000–18
Source: Deutsche Bundesbank (2000–18).

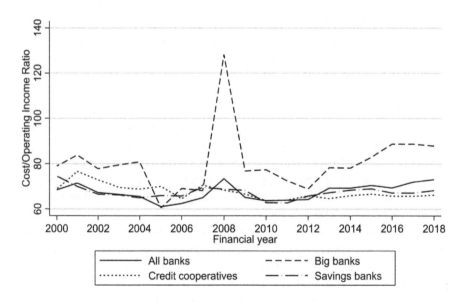

Figure 3.6 Cost/operating income ratio by bank type, 2000–18
Source: Deutsche Bundesbank (2000–18).

Table 3.1 Sparkassen aggregate data, 2007–18

Year	Sparkassen	Employees	Branches	Assets/ Employees	Total Assets
2007	446	253,696	15,932	4,119	€1,044,962,243
2008	438	251,400	15,812	4,259	€1,070,749,002
2009	431	249,577	15,697	4,301	€1,073,323,317
2010	429	248,081	15,626	4,371	€1,084,336,387
2011	426	245,969	15,446	4,464	€1,097,955,777
2012	423	244,862	15,295	4,516	€1,105,784,732
2013	417	244,038	15,095	4,555	€1,111,570,906
2014	416	240,146	14,872	4,695	€1,127,465,680
2015	413	233,741	14,451	4,900	€1,145,339,889
2016	403	224,671	13,779	5,221	€1,173,108,633
2017	390	216,117	13,316	5,552	€1,199,905,304
2018	385	209,588	13,016	5,932	€1,243,299,604

Source: DSGV 2000-2018. Sparkassenrangliste.

buses (Strotmann 2019). And mostly importantly, Sparkassen reduced the number of employees by 17 per cent from 2007 to 2018. What is striking is that the cost-cutting and efficiency gains occurred at the same time as savings banks' asset portfolio increased by 19 per cent. In other words, over the 12-year period Sparkassen did significantly more with less.

The trend in cost efficiency is also reflected in the ratio of assets to employees. The assets held by Sparkassen (loans, bonds, securities, cash) offer a proxy of business activity. In 2007 the ratio of assets to employees was €4,119, meaning there was one employee for every €4,119 worth of assets held by Sparkassen. By 2019 there was one Sparkassen employee for every €5,932 worth of assets, a 44 per cent improvement in efficiency. Furthermore, the number of employees per Sparkassen decreased from 569 employees per Sparkassen in 2010 to 544 employees per institution in 2018, a decline of 4 per cent.

In short, just as their profitability is surprising, the efficiency of Sparkassen defies expectations. The large public choice and economic literature on public banking argues public savings banks should be less efficient than private banks.

Moreover, the external challenges faced by all banks since the financial crisis should put a premium on economies of scale and size. Yet again, Sparkassen's experience since the 2007/08 financial crisis defies expectations. Public savings banks remain consistently more efficient than the commercial banking pillar and their efficiency has grown over time.

The puzzle

The preceding discussion frames the central puzzle of this book: what explains the resilience of Germany's public savings banks? Beneath the topic are three specific questions. First, what explains Sparkassen's remarkable performance? Or, how have they managed their gains in profitability and efficiency even in an environment that by all accounts should favour the large private banks?

More than two hundred years since their creation, Germany's public savings banks' business model and balance sheets remain largely unchanged: liabilities consist mainly of small depositors and assets comprise mainly of loans to individuals, small businesses and governments. In addition, the credit institutions have remained small and local. In 2018 the median-size public savings bank held $1.7 billion[13] in assets (DSGV 2018). By contrast JP Morgan Holdings, the largest US bank and HSBC Holdings, Europe's largest bank, held assets of $2,500 billion and $2,244 billion, respectively. Yet, despite the fact they retain what researchers describe as a "boring" business model (Schackmann-Fallis *et al.* 2017) and are significantly smaller than most commercial banks, the data paint a preliminary picture that is surprising and anachronistic: small independent public credit institutions whose business model follows a template established more than 200 years ago continue to play an outsized role in the largest economy in Europe. For anyone interested in banking and finance, or governments' role in influencing local economies, Germany's public savings banks stand out as something to be explained. Their resilience and success in the twenty-first century are particularly surprising given scholarly and periodic accounts of how Germany's banking system should have developed in the past two decades.

A second question centres on Sparkassen's performance during the financial crisis. Although they are not profit-maximizing entities, Sparkassen are nevertheless run as for-profit businesses. Their balance sheets reflect their business success. Yet, how did Germany's public savings banks avoid the pitfalls that led to the financial crisis? The regulatory environment of the three pillars of Germany's bank system is the same. Sparkassen are subject to the same regulations as other banks. Yet while Germany's commercial banks and Landesbanken gorged themselves on the mortgage-backed securities linked to the US housing market, Sparkassen largely kept their distance. Sparkassen chose not to make bets on the opaque derivatives that yielded extraordinary returns but ultimately lead to equally spectacular losses. What kept Sparkassen from making the same mistakes as the other banks?

A final question that emerges from the preceding discussion is: how have Sparkassen managed to survive and thrive while savings banks in other countries disappeared or are transformed into entities indistinguishable from commercial banks? Across Europe, member states passed legislation that helped commercial banks often at the expense of local public savings banks. EU banking union is a project designed to improve and promote European banking but its success comes at the expense of local public banks. Countries like France, Spain and England have all passed legislation that undermined public savings banks. It is hardly a surprise that Europe has lost most of its public savings banks. This is a global phenomenon. US banking is now dominated by a small number of large institutions: JPMorgan Chase has $2.62 trillion in assets, Bank of America has $2.34 trillion, and Citigroup Inc. has $1.93 trillion (Hall 2019). With an average $1.6 billion in assets, Germany's public savings banks constitute rounding errors for most of their commercial bank competitors. How are Germany's public banks able to survive let alone thrive in an environment dominated by too-big-to-fail institutions? How have Germany's local public banks managed to compete? How have they managed to avoid or prevent the types of policies and laws that weaken small local credit institutions in other countries? In short, what explains Sparkassen's resilience?

The answer developed in the following chapters is three-fold: first, Sparkassen's unique economic contribution to Germany's economy coupled with the symbiotic relationship to the local economies offers the most direct answer for the continued resilience of public savings banks. A second explanation is organization and in particular, the network within which savings banks are embedded and the institutional protection scheme that offers a more effective alternative to traditional deposit insurance. And finally, a third factor is politics and power, namely the ability of Germany's public savings banks to generate influence within domestic and international policy systems.

4

ECONOMIC EXPLANATIONS

"The health of the bank and the health of the region are intertwined. The causal arrow goes both ways." – Sparkassen CEO

What explains Sparkassen's remarkable staying power? How have these small independent credit institutions managed to weather the turbulent storms that led to the transformation, consolidation, or elimination of similar credit institutions in other countries? This chapter turns to economics to explain Sparkassen's resilience.

Much of our understanding links the success or failure of banking to the national or global economy. Greater globalization in trade and finance, for example, is often cited as a causal factor in the demise of community banks and the rise of banks so large they are too big to fail. National depressions, recessions, and economic booms are often linked to transformations in banking. In the case of Germany, the so-called "economic miracle" during the 1950s and 1960s generated significant productivity, much of it fueled by the expansion of Sparkassen lending to firms and individuals (Edwards & Fischer 1996). Since the 2007/08 financial crisis, Germany's economy went from "the sick man of Europe to Superstar" (Dustmann *et al.* 2014), also fueled in large part by bank loans, which originated with Sparkassen. Macroeconomic explanations, however, beg the question as to why Germany's savings banks survived even as public savings banks in other advanced industrialized countries that experienced similar economic growth did not. Macroeconomic accounts also fail to explain why, particularly in recent years, savings banks performed better than Germany's two other pillars – cooperatives and commercial banks. While all banking is affected by national and global events, for Sparkassen, local economic factors play a central role in their survival.

Given their "boring" business model – taking deposits and making loans – Sparkassen's staying power is a function of the economic value banks provide their local customers, particularly firms. This chapter explores Sparkassen's value-added to local economies and the relationship between bank performance and the financial health of a region. The chapter divides the topic into three sections. The first offers context into the relationship between banks and firms in Germany. Banks play a unique role in Germany's "managed" or "coordinated" system of capitalism (Lütz 2000; Hall & Soskice 2001). The section offers a brief primer on banking in Germany and Sparkassen's role within the country's economic system. A second section takes a deep dive into how stakeholders in communities value Sparkassen. Relational banking is the foundation of Sparkassen's economic value to local economies, and it is what sustains them.

A final section draws again on scholarly research to analyse the relationship between Sparkassen performance and the economic strength of the local economies. Given their economic value to firms and communities, one would expect a strong positive correlation between the economic health of a region and the economic health of the Sparkasse. The research suggests that while economics matters in explaining the resiliency of public savings banks, other factors may play a more critical role.

Sparkassen and Germany's economic system

Although they have been around since the eighteenth century, economists and political economists have only recently begun studying Sparkassen's contributions to Germany's economy. Most of the attention to banking and finance in Germany has historically concentrated on the handful of large commercial banks and their close relationship to the country's vast industrial sectors – steel, automobiles and energy. The origins of German banking and finance are linked to the country's effort to catch up to the United Kingdom and the United States in the second half of the nineteenth century. German industry required significant capital investment to pay for steel mills and large industrial factories, financial investments that could only be provided through a handful of large commercial banks (Gerschenkron 1962). The need for capital led to the emergence of so-called Hausbanks, which lent money to firms but then took equity positions in companies, served on supervisory boards, and played an active role in firm management and governance. As US companies turned to the stock markets to fund investment, the close relationship between Hausbanks and industry became the template for German's economy moving forward. Scholars like Hilferding (1910), Gerschenkron (1962), and Shonfield (1969) pin the birth of modern German capitalism on the enormous concentrations of economic power and the close industry–banking relationship. Rather than equity markets driving financial decision-making, it was the "bank-industrial oligopoly" that directed the course of Germany's economic development (Deeg 1999: 10). The primacy of large commercial banks to Germany's economic success went largely unquestioned until Richard Deeg's work (1999).

While large-scale industrial production was an essential aspect of Germany's economic modernization story, Deeg pointed out that an equally important part of Germany's economic story is the development of small and medium-sized firms (SMEs) known in German as the Mittelstand. In the late nineteenth century, Mittelstand firms consisted of artisans, shopkeepers, and peasants who relied on craft-based systems of production (as opposed to mass-production techniques). As industrialization grew in large urban areas, Mittelstand firms remained an essential source of economic activity throughout the rest of the country. These nineteenth century and early twentieth century SMEs were considered a model of economic and social discipline, and the guarantors of social and economic stability (Lane & Quack 1999). The Mittelstand was, "a group captured neither by the reckless spirit of laissez-faire capitalism nor the 'class hatred' of the workers" (Blackbourn 1977: 412).

Today, Mittelstand firms are family-owned or family-controlled companies that employ less than 500 employees or earn less than €50 million in annual revenue. Politicians, journalists and scholars view SMEs as the "backbone of Germany's economy" because they comprise 99 per cent of all companies, employ 70 per cent of the labour force and generate 1 out of every 2 euros of productivity in the country (Herr & Nettekoven 2018; *The Economist* 2014; Randow & Kirchfeld 2010; Simon 2017; BMWi 2018). Germany's "hidden champions" are SMEs that compete globally by producing high value-added products and services (Audretsch *et al*. 2018).

Moreover, while large industrial firms are concentrated in a handful of cities, Germany's SMEs are spread throughout the country in urban and rural regions, as well as areas underserved by commercial banks. SMEs' geographic distribution ensures the economic benefits of productivity and wealth creation are not concentrated in a handful of cities but spread throughout the country (Klagge *et al*. 2017).

SMEs' global competitiveness is attributed to their size, razor-thin margins, skilled labour force, and export-oriented business model (Pahnke & Welter 2019). SMEs are considered to be nimble, efficient and flexible. But perhaps the most critical component of SMEs' success is their financing. During the nineteenth century, when large industrial companies formed Hausbank relationships with large commercial banks, SMEs developed close ties with their local Sparkasse and cooperatives (Krahnen & Schmidt 2004). Sparkassen did not take an equity stake in firms or play the same active role in firm management that the large banks did. However, Sparkassen played a Hausbank role: developing close formal and informal relations, sharing information, and offering a variety of services tailored to the specific needs of the company.

Over time, the Hausbank–firm relationship became more myth than reality among large corporations and large banks (Edwards & Fischer 1996). Globalization and financialization led large companies to finance investment through sources other than commercial banks. And large commercial banks like Deutsche Bank shifted from traditional firm lending to investment banking and securities trading activities. However, the Sparkassen–SME relationship not only remained steady but grew throughout the postwar period. In the 1980s and 1990s, the link became particularly crucial as SMEs sought to compete on global markets by increasing their investment in research and development, training, and new production techniques described by Wolfgang Streeck as "diversified quality production" (DQP) systems (Streeck 1992). Financing from Sparkassen was instrumental in enabling SMEs to make the long-term investments necessary to transition from domestic-oriented family businesses to the "hidden champions" able to compete on the global stage (Deeg 1999; Berghoff 2006; Klagge *et al.* 2017; Fritsch & Wyrwich 2020).

The relationship between Sparkassen and SMEs was strengthened further after the financial crisis of 2007/08 when large commercial banks and regional public banks cut back on their lending. When the recession hit, commercial banks reduced the capital available to firms, called in loans, and tightened up lending requirements. SMEs turned to Sparkassen and cooperatives for help. The public savings banks responded to the financial crisis by turning on the tap and increasing their lending to SMEs and extending the length of their loans, which bolstered SMEs' ability to weather the economic storm. Lending by Sparkassen at the peak of the financial crisis in 2008 rose by nearly €14 billion (*Der Tagesspiegel* 2009), just as commercial banks were scaling back. Several Sparkassen managers who served as bank CEOs during the financial crisis said the financial crisis was a boom for the public savings banks. Return-on-equity spiked in 2010 and, after dropping slightly, remained consistently higher than that of commercial banks or cooperatives. One CEO, who heads a savings bank in eastern Germany, looked almost guilty when asked about the financial crisis:

> The crisis was a huge opportunity for us. Our competitors – private banks and Landesbanken – were dealing with their problems and had to cut back on their activities. We are a bank with healthy reserves that did not make the same risky bets as our larger competitors. As a result, we were able to consistently expand our credit business and increase our customers, many of whom had worked with private banks who just wanted a business partner they could count on.

The Sparkassen's action occurred at the very moment SMEs needed access to credit most. Another CEO noted that Sparkassen were more likely than their private competitors to practice forbearance during a recession: "We are much more likely to extend the length of the loan for one of our customers who is hurt by the recession because we have known them for a long time and because if their business fails, it might have a detrimental effect on the entire community." Expanding their lending during and after the financial crisis helped SMEs and helped to stabilize the economy. In the end, the financial crisis further strengthened the close connection between small firms and their Sparkasse.

The obvious question that emerges is: what do Sparkassen offer SMEs? It is clear that Sparkassen and SMEs enjoy a kind of Hausbank relationship, but what does the relationship mean in practice? And why does the relationship continue when Germany's banking market is more competitive than ever, and interest rates are at the lowest? Why do SMEs turn to local public savings banks for credit even when other financial institutions might offer better prices? The next section draws on the first-hand experiences of Sparkassen managers, customers, and community leaders to tackle these questions.

Sparkassen and the economics of relational banking

Savings banks' economic value stems from their close long-term relationship with the SMEs in their community. A Sparkassen manager stated, "The relationship we have with our customers and clients is who we are. Our employees work and live in the community, we are one of the largest taxpayers and employers in the community, and we fund a big part of the civic life of the community through our foundations." The quote underscores that the relationship is perceived by stakeholders to go in both directions: the bank trusts and benefits from the community and the community trusts and benefits from the firm. The *Financial Times* reported in 2019 that when a family-owned mineral water company, Stiftsquelle, relocated its headquarters to a new region of the country, it retained its local savings bank (Storbeck 2019). Sebastian Brodmann, who runs the firm, acknowledged that he could have banked with a different financial institution, but "we have been clients of Sparkasse Essen since before the [second world] war". That loyalty is the result of the company's long-term relationship with its Sparkasse. And according to the *Financial Times*, the mutual trust between Sparkassen and their business clients, which develops over many years, is what enables Sparkassen to remain resilient and compete with larger commercial banks like Deutsche Bank and Commerzbank (Storbeck 2019). In response to the question "what does a Sparkasse offer SMEs?" a Sparkassen CEO stated:

> The absolute most crucial factor that stands at the top of what customers want is that their banks know them personally ... In business today,

no one has any time … If a customer calls me and says they need 100,000 euros for 30 days in their savings account in order to pay a bill, what do they expect of me? What do I expect from them? Do I say 'I need a copy of your balance sheet, and how is your wife?' No, I say, 'Of course. No problem. In one hour, the money will be in the account'… I can do this so efficiently because there is this trust that comes from knowing the customer and his firms inside and out for so long … It is extremely efficient. I trust him, and he knows he can count on this bank, particularly when things are tight financially.

The mutual trust between SMEs and their Hausbanks is referred to as "relational banking" (Deeg 2010; Hackenthal 2004). It essentially means that the bank and SME enjoy a long-term relationship in which they know and trust one another in good times as well as bad.

While relational banking declined in importance for large corporations and large commercial banks, it remains influential among local public savings banks for several reasons. First, Sparkassen's long history in providing SMEs with access to credit was cited by several stakeholders. Respondents note that private banks, particularly foreign- and internet-banks, "come and go", weakening their connections to clients. And large domestic, commercial banks are perceived as erratic and unstable. Deutsche Bank, for example, launched an aggressive initiative to enter into the retail banking market in 2008 but then later pulled back (Coppola 2015). "Deutsche Bank constantly changes its business model", said one local official adding, "people here do not know what business Deutsche Bank is in". Large commercial banks like Commerzbank and Deutsche Bank are viewed with particular scepticism in the eastern half of the country. Although they entered the eastern German market even before the Berlin Wall fell in 1989, commercial banks pulled back from the region in the 1990s, closing offices and branches, and leaving SMEs and governments looking for access to capital. Sparkassen (along with cooperatives), on the other hand, are pillars of stability and consistency. Savings banks continue to have offices or branches in nearly every county in the country, and their importance, particularly in financially underserved regions, has increased (Bresler *et al.* 2006).

Sparkassen's system of governance also fosters relational banking. Local political leaders sit on the supervisory boards of savings banks. And while such a close relationship between politicians and local public banks is viewed with scepticism by some (Hallerberg & Markgraf 2018), stakeholders noted that the governance structure bolsters trust between the bank and community. Political leaders and bank managers view the supervisory board as an institution where information and concerns about credit to SMEs are shared, which, in turn, fosters mutual trust between the bank, government and local firms.

Sparkassen's business model and mission also help explain the resilience of relational banking. By constraining Sparkassen to make loans and take deposits within a single jurisdiction, the regional principle incentivizes savings banks to build and nurture strong relations with the local community. Bank managers repeatedly stressed that the health of savings banks depends on the banks' close relationship with the local community. Also, unlike US credit institutions, German savings banks retain the loans they make rather than sell or securitize them. Retention of their loans creates a further incentive for the bank to care about the long-term health of their SME borrower since the banks' revenue depends on interest payments and future borrowing, not commissions. A savings bank manager shared that in the wake of the financial crisis, he had to reassure all of his clients that the bank would never sell their loans. "For them", the bank manager said, "it is a matter of trust. If we had sold their loan to another entity, it would have undermined their faith in us."

A final factor that contributes to the stability of relational banking is the savings banks' mission. "We are for-profit, but we are not profit-maximizing", one bank manager said. Among the most critical elements of the Sparkassen's mission is providing firms and individuals in their community with access to credit. A manager from a regional Sparkassen association said that while there are differences across banks and regional associations, "we all have the same goals and business models. What unifies us is providing financial services for our region, guaranteeing financing for SMEs, giving all societal groups banking services, being present in our region, and close to our customers." Savings banks have a statutory requirement to provide access to banking and credit to SMEs and individuals in their region. This includes access for refugees from Syria and Afghanistan, who sought asylum in Germany in 2016 (Arnold 2016). Savings banks extend credit and banking services to customers, even at the expense of revenues. The bank does this because it fulfills its mix of public and private purposes.

Moreover, stakeholders note that when a Sparkasse offers a loan to an SME, it strengthens the relationship between bank and client, and raises the bank's profile and trust within the broader community. As a local business person noted, "People talk. We are a small community. We know when the Sparkasse supports a new development or helps local businesses. The information gets around quickly."

In short, relational banking sets Sparkassen apart from commercial banks. Cooperative banks share many of the same features, but they are significantly smaller. Furthermore, relational banking is not the natural outcome of market forces. Instead, relational banking is sustained through several factors that include: Sparkassen's historic commitment to underserved regions of the country, their system of governance; their business model; and local savings banks' public/private mission. But what economic benefits flow from relational banking?

Political economic literature and interviews with stakeholders, point to two benefits that SMEs receive from relational-banking: stable long-term credit, and market and managerial information (Deeg 1999; Zysman 1994; Deeg & Donnelly 2016).

Long-term credit

Sparkassen stakeholders and managers emphasize access to long-term credit – so-called "patient capital" – as a central economic value produced by relational banking (Deeg 1999; Lütz 2000). Firms, regardless of size, require capital. To cover their financial needs, firms can borrow from banks or issue debt securities such as bonds on capital markets. Either option works; however, for SMEs borrowing from Sparkassen offers significant advantages to issuing bonds on a capital market: lower disclosure costs; avoidance of external ratings which bond issuers require; and saving on expenses associated with issuing or placing a bond. Borrowing as opposed to issuing bonds also allows firms to borrow at much smaller volumes, which is particularly attractive to SMEs (Schackmann-Fallis *et al.* 2017). Sparkassen offer SMEs long-term loans at competitive rates because of how relational banking solves specific information asymmetries between banks and clients.

Regardless of whether financing occurs through a bank loan or a bond, the bank or capital investor knows less about the firm than the firm itself. There is thus an information asymmetry: the SME knows more than the bank or investor. The greater the asymmetry, the higher the risk. The price of the loan or the bond reflects that risk. Information asymmetries are particularly acute in the case of capital markets where investors are often legally prevented from gaining "inside" information about a company. And companies have an incentive to withhold negative information about a firm for fear investors might panic and drive down the value of the firm. It places a premium on the capacity of corporate regulators like the Securities and Exchange Commission to ensure companies remain transparent about their finances (Khademian 1992). Moreover, information asymmetries make capital markets vulnerable to a herd-like mentality in which bond yields often reflect rumours rather than reality (Tversky & Kahneman 1992).

Information asymmetries and moral hazard issues also characterize bank lending. Borrowers know more about their willingness and ability to pay than lenders. The information asymmetry leads banks to misprice loans or make loans they should reject. The problem is particularly severe whenever a bank purchases another bank; the new larger entity lacks the information about its customers (Alessandrini *et al.* 2008). Furthermore, the information asymmetries increase as the size of the company gets smaller (Schackmann-Fallis *et al.* 2017). Smaller

SMEs often lack specific financial knowledge and expertise, documentation and record-keeping are not as systematized, and the low volume of loans makes it less profitable to issue a credit, leading banks to charge a risk premium, which further weakens SMEs' competitiveness.

Sparkassen, by contrast, because they share a close and long-term relationship with firms, overcome the information asymmetries that plague capital markets and Anglo-Saxon models of banking. As a result, Sparkassen offer longer-term loans to SMEs, which lowers the cost of the loans and provides firms with stability. A 2012 Deutsche Bundesbank report noted, "Long-term lending relationships, frequently with one bank ... meant that banks in Germany, in contrast to capital providers with less close business relationships with enterprises, frequently had privileged access to information, enabling them to assess the enterprise's economic situations adequately ... This also had a positive effect on enterprises' financing costs" (Deutsche Bundesbank 2012: 21). In the early 2000s, credit to SMEs was cut when banks were forced to comply with new Basel II regulations that called for a stricter credit standard (Deutsche Bundesbank 2005). The financial crisis and the European debt crisis led to an even more significant tightening of credit across banks. Yet, despite stricter standards and much worry, SMEs were spared mainly from a credit crunch in the mid-2000s (Deutsche Bundesbank 2005) and after the financial crisis (Schmidt & Zwick 2012). The reason credit rationing did not occur is because of relational banking. Sparkassen's Hausbank model kept credit flowing and stabilized distressed SMEs because, "a banker who knows his region and the people faces smaller information asymmetries and might be more willing to offer financial services to this special group" (Bresler 2006: 260; Elsas & Krahnen 2004). In 2019, stakeholders involved in financing SMEs concurred with Bresler *et al.* (2006) findings in the early 2000s: the close and long-term relationship between savings banks and SMEs is what banks offer firms.

In interviews, Sparkassen managers and SME customers underscore what overcoming information asymmetries looks like in practice. According to respondents, because of the socio-cultural and geographical closeness to their clients' savings, banks can take into account "soft information factors" (Schackmann-Fallis *et al.* 2017; DeYoung *et al.* 2008). As one SME manager put it, "the Sparkassen knows that the company director just lost his wife or that there is an illness in the family. They take this personnel knowledge into account when deciding on a loan or the terms of a loan." And because they have access to internal information about a firm's management, banks are more willing to support longer-term loans at attractive interest rates, more readily refinance clients facing a financial crisis, and reduce the incentives to speculate (Lütz 2000; Crouch & Streeck 1997).

Bank customers also stressed the importance of not only having a banker they trust but also a bank employee with authority to act. "With the larger private banks", said one SME customer, "managers have to check with Frankfurt first [their headquarters], but the Sparkassen manager knows me and can make a decision immediately that can help me". Moreover, state statutes require Sparkassen to put the economic needs of their communities and the welfare of SMEs above the pursuit of profitability (Stern 1984). A Sparkassen manager cited an automobile supplier in his region, "The auto supplier's success affects other companies in the city, many of whom also do business with the Sparkasse". In other words, savings banks take into account the impact of the SME customer to the broader community when making lending decisions, further strengthening the level of trust between the bank and the community. Besides long-term financing, Sparkassen stakeholders also point out the informational role the banks play for firms and leaders in the region.

Market and managerial information

Sparkassen and SMEs are part of local economic networks that consist not only of banks and firms but also trade associations, federal and state agencies, local governments, and Chambers of Industry, Handicraft, and Commerce. The network consists of formal and informal relationships that coordinate economic activities in ways that reduce the risk to banks and affect the financing of SMEs (Lane & Quack 1999). Christel Lane's (1995) work, for example, shows the role that Chambers of Industry play in reducing business failures by providing SMEs, particularly start-ups, with training and expertise, which in turn lowers bank risks. Respondents report that local government officials work with savings bank leaders to plan local infrastructure projects such as a new school or community centre or business development, which in turn reduces the risk to banks.

Much of the market and managerial information is produced by Sparkassen and shared within the network. The shared information enables network actors to understand the needs of SMEs and the likely effect of different types of intervention in the local economy. According to respondents, Sparkassen and their managers are at the centre of these local economic networks described by Lane and Quack and others. Their place within the network is partly a function of the banks' business model, the regional principle and their closeness to the community, and the structure of the banks' supervisory boards, which include local politicians. Scholars commonly reference these factors. However, another essential factor emerged from interviews: savings banks' multifaceted presence within the community.

Sparkassen CEOs and their management teams serve on a variety of local supervisory boards, including boards overseeing hospitals and public housing authorities. Managers reference their role in local business associations and leadership roles in local clubs and associations. Moreover, the Sparkasse CEOs interviewed had all been in their positions for nearly two decades, giving them creditability among politicians and business leaders in the community. Also, the public perceives savings banks as apolitical since they work with (and for) governments, are overseen by every local political coalition, and engage with all interests within the local economic network. Savings banks also contribute financially to hundreds of civil society organizations in their communities through charity work. That means that savings banks are connected to all aspects of social life in the community, further facilitating communication flows. And finally, as several bank managers pointed out, "We are the centre of the community". It is thus not surprising that a Sparkasse CEO echoed the sentiment expressed by every CEO in discussing his banks' role in the community, "We regard ourselves as the centre of the financial circle in the community". But what does that mean in practice? What does it mean to be in the centre of the local economic network?

First, it means savings banks coordinate and share information with local governments over a variety of economic and financial issues in the local community. Several Sparkassen managers referenced their involvement in their local government's economic development plans, including a new business park, "There's no development that happens in this city that we do not know about, and we're involved in most of them". Local governments are also free to bank with any financial institution. However, governments rely primarily on Sparkassen for the lending and depository needs. In recent years, local governments turned to auctions for their credit needs, asking banks to bid on loans to governments. Bank managers note loans to governments are less attractive than they once were because the interest rates charged to public entities are so low. One manager said, "It's not worth it for us to offer our local governments credit. They can get it elsewhere." Nevertheless, governments run most of their financial transactions through the local savings banks, and they keep their deposits in the local savings banks. And finally, savings banks and governments coordinate a great deal to resolve public problems and crises such flooding, helping refugees with access to banking services, or ensuring that firms have access to credit and customers access to banking services during the Covid-19 pandemic.

Being at the centre of a local economic network also means savings banks consult with their SME customers. Sparkassen have the advantage of being small and local as well as large and national. The capacity to be small and big at the same time enables savings banks to offer SMEs advice that reflects an intimate knowledge of the local political and economic context. At the same time, savings banks can draw on an enormous S-Group database to provide SMEs with useful analyses for their business. One SME client said that his Sparkasse provided his firm with a list of suppliers, a review of the local labour market, and an analysis of his company's entire sector. A Sparkassen CEO noted that because most German SMEs borrow from Sparkassen, the banks know a great deal about products, prices and supply chains for nearly every industry. A savings bank CEO gave the example of a small manufacturing firm, "Consulting means that in good times and bad we talk to our clients about the state of things … as a part of the S-Group, we have an incredible wealth of experience. We know how certain things work because we see how the entire industry works. So if our client sets prices that are way off the mark for the industry, we let them know." Similarly, if a client seeks a new line of credit to expand production capacity or work on a new project, the bank CEOs said that they can efficiently and accurately evaluate the business plan and the projected numbers because "there is a strong chance that we [Sparkassen] did similar deals in other places".

In short, the ability to provide long-term credit and valuable managerial and sectoral information to SMEs in their community illustrates the central role Sparkassen play not just in the local economies but in Germany's unique form of capitalism. Local economic development occurs not as a result of a tax abatement or a financial handout to firms that play governments off of each other. Instead, economic growth is the result of a coordinated network of local actors sharing information and providing access to consistent long-term credit. Local politicians are involved. However, government involvement is indirect and within the network. As Wolfgang Streeck (1992) notes, local governments do not need to provide assistance to firms directly. Instead, local officials influence firms indirectly through behavioural regulation of the market participants that create obligations for cooperative behaviour.

With a clear understanding of the economic value Sparkassen add to local communities, the next section turns to the relationship between the health of the region and the health of the Sparkassen.

Bank-region connection

The most proximate economic explanation for Sparkassen's resilience and survival may be the economic health of their jurisdiction. The preceding sections underscore the economic value public savings banks add to SMEs and local communities. And, as noted in Chapter 2, public savings banks' business model is relatively simple and reminiscent of Savings and Loans' business model in the United States before deregulation in the 1980s. Sparkassen take in deposits from customers in their region and lend those deposits out to borrowers, individuals and businesses in the region looking to purchase a home or grow a business. The net difference in the interest rate of deposits and loans is the revenue that fuels the banks' business. Moreover, there is usually an overlap between depositors and borrowers: those who take out a loan also have a savings account with the institution. Sparkassen also adhere to a strict regional principle, which limits banks from conducting business outside an area typically the size of one or two counties. One would expect a connection or "synergy" as one respondent described it between the economic health of the Sparkasse and the economic health of the local region.

Under this theory, Sparkassen located in regions that are poorer and less populated may be more vulnerable and less profitable since there are fewer potential depositors, fewer businesses and less borrowing. More impoverished regions are also likely to be associated with higher default rates and greater risk to banks. This could be particularly the case in parts of eastern Germany that are poorer and have lost population. On the other hand, Sparkassen located in wealthier and more populated areas, should do very well financially. Greater wealth and population density mean more depositors and more borrowing by firms and individuals. One might also expect lower default rates and, thus, a more economically stable financial institution. Therefore, the most direct explanation for Sparkassen's success or failure should be the economic health of the region in which they are located.

Economists have examined this relationship for more than a decade and come to the surprising conclusion that the relationship between bank and region is tenuous at best (Christians 2015; Gärtner 2008, 2017; Gärtner & Christians 2015; Tischer 2011). While the largest public savings banks are located in the largest and wealthiest cities in Germany, the Great Recession demonstrated that size or asset volume alone is by no means synonymous with stability or profitability. Moreover, research on the connection between bank and region finds little support for claims that savings banks survive and thrive because their region's economy does well. The picture is far more complicated.

Stefan Gärtner (2008), for example, developed a measure of Sparkassen health (0 to 1) by combining factors such as cost-to-income ratios, reserve levels and operating profits. He then developed a measure of regional economic health (0 to 1) combining factors such as loss of population, unemployment, local GDP and percentage of the population in technical professions. Figure 4.1 is taken from Gärtner's research and the findings are somewhat counter intuitive. The stronger the bank the higher the number. The weaker region the higher the number. The scatter plot image shows a spurious relationship between each Sparkasse and its local region's economic strength from 1999 to 2003.

The relationship between banks and their regions is all over the map. Indeed, the trendline indicates the opposite of what one would expect; more profitable Sparkassen are in more impoverished and less populated areas of the country. Banks lend more in wealthier regions of the country. Savings banks with higher reserves and higher profits are located in poorer regions of the country. Overall the relationship is extremely weak and tends in the opposite direction of what we

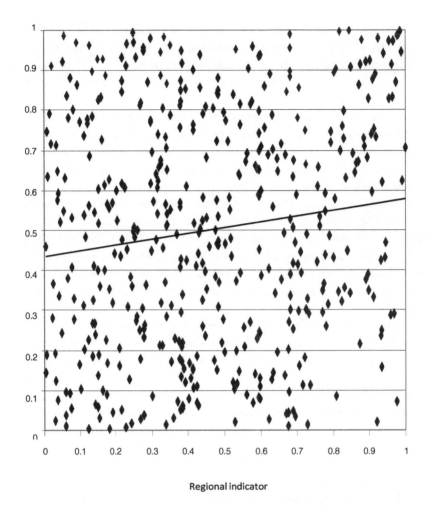

Figure 4.1 Relationship between Sparkassen profitability and regional economic health
Note: The stronger the economic health of the bank, the higher the Sparkassen indicator; the weaker a region is economically, the higher the regional indicator.
Source: cited in Gärtner (2010: 213).

might expect. Gärtner speculates the reason for the surprising outcome is that poorer areas have higher reserves because they lend less and are more risk-averse. It's also possible that savings banks in poorer regions are more profitable because they invest more of their deposits in funds and investments outside the region.

Tischer (2011) and Gärtner and Christians (2015) study the health of Sparkassen within regional clusters and find that the economic health of a region or its population loss/gain does little to account for a Sparkasse's health. A high volume of lending characterizes wealthier areas. However, the net-interest rate margins in high-density regions are lower. In other words, the difference between what banks pay depositors and charge lenders is narrower in more prosperous and high-density regions. Competition is also higher in more populated and wealthier regions, cutting further into profitability.

Tischer (2011) examines Sparkassen from 1994 to 2008 and finds public savings banks in poorer parts of the country, particularly in the east, are more efficient. They had lower administrative costs and lower cost-to-income ratios than their western counterparts. Like Gärtner, Tischer finds eastern banks rely more on commission income than interest income, which further increased their profitability.

A further factor is demography. Berlemann *et al.* (2014) note Germany's relatively low birth rate contributes to the health of Sparkassen. The older we are, the greater our earnings, assets and wealth. Financial institutions profit more from older people than the young. And in Germany, the elderly tend to live disproportionately in poorer and less dense parts of the country, and they are overwhelmingly loyal to Sparkassen. Demographic trends lead Oestmann (2014) to speculate that even in regions losing population, Sparkassen can still do well.

Interviews with stakeholders confirm much of the published research. Bank managers noted that Sparkassen in poorer regions of the country were able to invest excess reserves in funds that enabled them to manage their risk. The Sparkassen CEOs in poorer eastern regions of the country pointed out with some pride that they outperformed many of the savings banks located in wealthier regions of the country. They attribute their success to several factors not mentioned in the research. First, their mission to ensure access to banking services means that they provide the essential services people need in Germany. "Even poor people need a bank for their savings and their income. You cannot exist in Germany without a bank account. We service the needs of the 'normal citizen'", explained a CEO. Another factor is loyalty. Several managers and SME customers noted that there is a great deal of loyalty toward Sparkassen in the east in part because the savings banks had been the only financial institutions that existed in former East Germany. Particularly among the elderly in eastern Germany, the connection to Sparkassen remains strong. An additional factor referenced in comparing Sparkassen with other kinds of banks is administrative costs. Several representatives from the private banking sector made this point, "Bank employees and managers in Sparkassen earn a lot less than their counterparts in commercial banks. The salaries in the savings banks are lower, and therefore their costs are lower."

Finally, every stakeholder within the S-Group (not surprisingly) underscored the role management plays in the success of the financial institutions. The leader at the DSGV captures the sentiment: "The profitability of the Sparkasse has little to do with the profitability or development of the region. We have tried to find a correlation, and there simply isn't one! The factors that contribute to the profitability of the Sparkasse are connected to the quality of the management and how well management implements the banks' business model."

The DSGV executive's comments underscore the findings of this chapter. Economics matters in explaining Sparkassen's resilience. The public savings banks succeed in part because of the role they have played historically and today in Germany's economic system, namely their Hausbank role to SMEs in the country. To stakeholders – SMEs, community leaders, government officials, bank managers – relational banking contributes to Sparkassen's value-added by offering long-term (patient) capital to SMEs at attractive rates, and by playing a central role in the creation and dissemination of market and managerial information. At the same time, the DSGV executive points out the success of any one savings bank is a function of a variety of factors. Even a region's wealth and productivity are a poor predictor of the banks' success. Economics contributes to the resiliency of Sparkassen, but economics is insufficient to explain how Sparkassen navigate a world of global financial capitalism in which institutions that are "too big to fail" seem ascendant.

The following chapters explore the administrative and political factors that also account for Sparkassen's resiliency.

5

ADMINISTRATIVE EXPLANATIONS

"Independence is a double-edged sword."– Sparkassen CEO

This chapter examines how administration contributes to Sparkassen's performance, accountability, and ability to survive in the too-big-to-fail world of global finance. As the preceding chapter argues, economic value and competitiveness are critical explanations for Sparkassen's resilience; they continue because they out-compete their rivals and serve the economic and social needs of their public sector owners/sponsors. But economic value alone does not account for Sparkassen's performance during the first two decades of the twenty-first century, a period that overlaps the worst banking crisis since the Great Depression. Before the financial crisis, private banks like Deutsche Bank and Lehman Brothers, regional public banks like WestLB and Sachsen LB, and even public savings banks like Spain's Cajas were competitive and added value for their customers and public and private sponsors/owners. Yet, the credit institutions which soared financially also suffered extraordinary losses, failed to recover, and, in some cases, went bankrupt. Germany's Sparkassen could have followed a similar path.

As independent universal banks, German public savings banks could have followed Landesbanken's lead and gambled on the opaque financial products that brought down the giant WestLB. Banking regulators, Sparkassen CEOs, and representatives of regional and national Sparkassen associations expressed a similar view: that if Sparkassen managers had wanted to purchase the same US mortgage-backed securities that sunk the biggest banks, the local savings banks were legally permitted to do so. One Sparkassen CEO from a small institution expressed the consensus:

> You have to understand, the management of a savings bank has a lot of power ... and a lot of options. Their independence is a double-edged sword. It's hugely beneficial to the business model because it supports relational banking and enables the bank to be flexible. At the same time,

independence allows individual banks to make poor choices too, including investment in risky securities.

Several Sparkassen CEOs interviewed for this research acknowledged feeling pressure from some of their peers and particularly their Landesbanken colleagues to invest in risky funds that promised high returns (Gubitz 2013). And indeed, several Sparkassen, particularly larger institutions like Nassauische Sparkasse in Frankfurt, not only set up failed subsidiaries in Ireland but also took a €42 million bite out of the Lehman Brothers' apple (Köhler 2011; Dönch et al. 2009; Siemens 2008). Yet, except for a small handful of Sparkassen, the vast majority of public savings banks resisted the temptation to follow in the footsteps of their larger public and private competitors (Bofinger et al. 2008; Semenyshyn 2017; Scherrer 2014; Hüfner 2010; Butzbach 2008). Only a small number of public savings banks lost money during the financial crisis. And, as shown in Chapter 3, public savings banks have done remarkably well since the crisis while fulfilling their public mandates. Finally, Sparkassen are among the most efficient banks in Germany. Germany's public savings banks in the aggregate spend significantly less on administrative costs than private banks.

What explains public savings banks' success and their restraint in the face of extraordinary pressure? What enables savings banks to compete and keeps them from making the same mistakes as their private and public competitors? What contributes to their level of efficiency? As has been mentioned, public choice scholars argue public organizations are prone to corruption and inefficiencies (Moe 1984; Niskanen 1971); as entities linked to local governments, some might expect savings banks to be susceptible to more abuse and risky decision-making than their private competitors. Indeed, comparative banking scholarship suggests that public banks are less productive and less efficient than private banks (La Porta et al. 2002) and particularly prone to abuse and corruption (Shleifer & Vishny 1994). And lack of experience with capital markets coupled with a public mandate should make saving bank managers more vulnerable to poor investment choices and mismanagement. So what explains their competitiveness, resilience and resistance to the temptations that brought down the more prominent players of the global financial system?

One answer is that Sparkassen managers are particularly wise and prudent. Several Sparkassen managers suggested their training at relatively small public banks made them more risk-averse than managers in private banks; that because a savings bank manager's business was deposits and lending and not capital markets, managers would not purchase complicated securities they did not understand. It is difficult to assess such agent-based claims in the aftermath of the financial crisis. Hindsight offers clarity. Indeed, Sparkassen respondents interviewed seem prudent and wise, but so did respondents who work in private banks and Landesbanken. And while individual agency likely explains some Sparkassen performance, there were savings bank managers who did purchase risky securities they did not understand. And savings bank managers in other countries, notably Spain and Italy, for example, also lost significant sums.

Moreover, if agents behaved prudently, the critical question is, why? Turning to the present, what enables Sparkassen managers to take the prudent less-travelled financial road even as larger, wealthier, more powerful institutions often do not? The answer is administration matters.

Administration impacts Sparkassen's resiliency in two ways. First, administration bolsters their competitive advantage (Choulet 2017). Sparkassen are embedded within one of the largest administrative networks on the planet. The network consists of an integrated web of 540 companies connected vertically at each level of governance and horizontally across every county and city in Germany. The highly decentralized network spans public and private actors and institutions and complements Germany's decentralized federalist structure of government. The network structure allows Sparkassen to be independent, small, and local while at the same time profiting from the economies of scale that come with membership of one of the largest financial networks in the world (Simpson 2013; Choulet 2017).

Second, the administrative network establishes a unique system of accountability and oversight. Sparkassen, like all German banks, are under the supervision of the Bundesbank, the Federal Financial Supervisory Authority, and the European Central Bank. However, Sparkassen are also overseen by ministries of finance within each German state (the so-called "Sparkassenaufsicht") and by a set of administrative structures within their network that makes sure savings banks pursue their prudent and boring business model while also fulfilling their public mandates.

Following this introductory section, a second section lays out what we know theoretically about what sets administrative networks apart from traditional forms of public and private administration. The S-Group network and the competitive advantages that derive from the network are discussed in a third section. A final section turns to the administrative structures within the S-Group that ensure savings banks pursue safe and sound banking practices while also fulfilling their public mandates.

What sets networks apart?

Sparkassen are embedded within the Sparkassen Financial Group network or S-Group. Before turning to what it means to be embedded in the S-Group, it is helpful to consider the ways networks differ from traditional bureaucracies or markets. What keeps a network together? And how do networks affect the behaviour and capacity of organizations like Sparkassen, which exist within them?

Network theory has been applied to a range of fields, including sociology, health, law, biology, computer science, and international relations (Newman 2010; Paár-Jákli 2014). Public administration scholars trace the beginning of network theory to Lawrence O'Toole's seminal 1997 article "Treating Networks Seriously". O'Toole defines a network as a structure of interdependence that involves multiple organizational actors. Entities within a network can be arranged in a variety of ways, but they are organized neither as a hierarchy nor as a market. No unit is necessarily subordinate to another. Instead, the glue that connects a networks' components includes informal bonds, exchange relations, shared norms, or coalitions based on common interests. The internal linkages pose a challenge for governing or steering a network. As O'Toole notes, in a network, "administrators cannot be expected to exercise decisive leverage by virtue of their formal position". Instead, success depends on managing the formal and informal interconnections among those who implement policies and programmes, connections which often lie outside the typical chain of command (Ruckdäschel 2015; Williamson 1994: 324; Sydow *et al.* 2011: 331).

Networks exist on a spectrum. At one end is a loose collection of actors (firms, agencies, associations) with diffuse and shifting memberships (Baker 1990). In such a diffuse network, public and private organizations collaborate not as part of the legally-defined structure but through mutual and predictable collaboration that advances member goals. At the other extreme, is a finite, closely-linked set of actors that maintain consistent and exclusive relationships with each other. In a formal network, like the S-Group, clear legal and functional lines delineate who is in and who is outside the network. A network contrasts sharply with a bureaucracy or market.

Max Weber's classic bureaucratic model views organizations through a hierarchical lens in which specific actors or units are formally connected, and each is responsible for particular activities (Gulick & Urwick 1937; Weber 1964). Accountability and performance are a function of a self-contained, top-down system with a transparent chain of command, limited spans of control, clear lines of authority, and formal separation between line and staff activities. Woodrow Wilson, former US president and political science professor, argued the classic model not only facilitates accountability and efficiency, but also promotes administrative values such as rationality, expertise and neutrality (Wilson 1887).

A network is also distinct from a market. Markets are atomistic structures in which firms and actors are connected through arm's-length exchanges (Hirschman 2004). Collusion or even coordination is discouraged or prohibited. Indeed, according to market theory, it is selfish, profit-maximizing behaviour that motivates arm's-length relationships (Lazonick 1991). Transactions are limited to the exchange of data on price, quality and (marginal) cost, which, assuming a competitive environment, is the only information needed to reach efficient decisions. Efficiency and accountability are achieved by ensuring equal access to markets (Uzzi 1996).

By contrast, actors within a network are also autonomous, but they are "embedded" within a network. Embeddedness means that "exchanges within a group ... have an ongoing social structure" (Marsden 1981: 1210, cited in Uzzi 1996). Network actors are neither subordinate to one another (as a hierarchical organization) nor atomistic. Network actors are independent, but they cooperate, share information, provide services to each other, and are connected through a set of similar goals and objectives. And while markets rely exclusively on price to determine value, units within a network often value outputs for which there may not be an obvious market or price. Sparkassen, for example, view profits and social outcomes as equally important even though the former may be easier to measure than the latter. Networks are thus fundamentally different from traditional bureaucratic or market models (Powell 1990). But what benefits do networks offer?

Network theory points to several advantages including shared labour and resource pools (Dyer & Singh 1998), increased innovativeness and flexibility (Eisingerich *et al.* 2010; Porter 2003), improved inter-organizational learning (Powell & Grodal 2006), and overall performance (Schilling & Phelps 2007; Cassiman *et al.* 2009). The research also emphasizes the advantages of smaller organizations. Administrative networks offer the chance for smaller enterprises to cost-efficiently acquire know-how and resources through cooperation with other entities within the network (Ruckdäschel 2015: 2; Westerlund 2010). The advantages described in network theory are evident in the case of Sparkassen and the S-Group.

The following section describes the Sparkassen's network and how administration bolsters their capacity and resilience.

Sparkassen's comparative advantage from the network

Sparkassen are embedded within S-Group, a network that consists of 540 companies with 17,500 branches, 300,000 employees, and €2.8 trillion in assets (Finanzgruppe Deutscher Sparkassen- und Giroverband 2018). It is among the largest financial networks in the world. Yet, what sets the S-Group apart from a holding company or corporation is less its size than its administrative structure. The S-Group is neither hierarchical nor market-based nor voluntary (Simpson 2013). It operates based on common interest and is held together by a combination of economic rationality, group philosophy, corporate identity, capital connections, and laws and regulations (Gärtner 2008). Cooperation within the network is characterized by close interaction of entities at three levels that fit comfortably within the country's federalist system.

Organisations of the Savings Banks Finance Group

The Savings Banks Finance Group[*]

Status 31.12.2019   • Not a representation of hierarchy or ownership structure

Sparkassen		Landesbanken		Regional Building Societies		Regional Public Insurance Groups	
Number of Institutions	379*	Number of LB Companies	5	Number of Institutions	8	Number	10
Total Assets	€1,301 Bn.	Total Assets**	€882 Bn.	Total Assets	€73 Bn.	Gross Premium Income	€22.2 Bn.
Employees	204,988	Employees	33,704	Employees - Internal	3,759	Employees - Internal	18,630
				Employees - External	3,199	Employees - External	9,330
* 378 as per 15.06.2020		**Excluding Deka/ incl. LB Berlin/ Berliner Sparkasse					

Equity Investment Companies		DekaBank German Giro Centre		S Rating und Risikosysteme		Regional Building Society Property Companies		Deutsche Leasing		Other Leasing Companies		Factoring Companies	
No. of Institutions	51	Total Assets	€97 Bn.			No. of Institutions	7	Total Assets	€22.1 Bn	New Business Volume	€2.1 Bn.	No. of Institutions	3
Investments	1,510					Vol. of Trade	€9.1 Bn.	New Business Volume	€10.3 Bn.			Annual Turnover	€31.8 Bn.
Total Vol.	€1.1 Bn.							Assets Under Management	€40.4 Bn.				
Employees	194	Employees	4,723	Employees	243	Employees Internal	124	Employees	2,624	Employees	726	Employees	387
						External	426						

Figure 5.1 Organization of the Savings Bank Finance Group
Source: Finanzgruppe Deutscher Sparkassen- und Giroverband 2020.

The network's first tier consists of the 385 Sparkassen or public savings banks that operate in nearly every county and city in Germany. As discussed previously, Sparkassen provide retail banking services for private clients, local companies and institutional customers. Sparkassen employ approximately 205,000 employees and hold around €1.3 trillion in assets. State laws restrict Sparkassen's business to a specific administrative jurisdiction, the so-called regional principle. As a result, Sparkassen do not compete with each other and are closely linked to their local government sponsors. What distinguishes Sparkassen further is their independence. Although limited to a specific region, each Sparkasse is free to do business the way it sees fit. A Sparkasse does not require permission from a central office, for example to issue credit or purchase a bond.

In an example of "institutional complementarity" (Deeg 2007) savings banks' independent structure complements the institutionalized system of local self-rule codified in Germany's Basic Law or constitution. Several respondents contrasted savings banks' structure with the Deutsche Bank to argue that savings banks fit with Germany's federalist system far better than private banks' organization. A representative from the cooperative banking sector, a competitor of Sparkassen, stated:

> In contrast to Deutsche Bank which was only interested in customers with large incomes, Sparkassen took the opposite approach. They wanted to do business with "normal" people. They went into the schools and communities, opened branches everywhere, were in the local clubs

... they are regionally incredibly strong. And don't forget, Germany is a federal state. The Savings Banks' decentralized structure, which annoys many outside of Germany, is compatible with the federalist structure of our government. We're not like France, where everything is centralized. Sparkassen, like our federal state, were deliberately decentralized.

At the state level, there are five Landesbanken, eight regional building societies, and 11 regional public insurance groups. With nearly €1 trillion in assets, the five Landesbanken are the most important state-level entities within the network. They are partially owned by a mix of state governments and regional savings banks associations.

Landesbanken historically have three functions. They serve as the house bank to their states by providing loans and cash management services. Second, they act as the central banks to the Sparkassen in the region, thus managing savings banks' cheque payments and cash transfer systems, liquidity needs and long-term lending. And finally, they provide commercial and investment banking services to domestic and foreign banks, non-banks and public clients (Gubitz 2013; Brämer *et al.* 2010). The close relationship with Landesbanken enables Sparkassen to offer their corporate banking clients underwriting services, derivative hedges, large or syndicated loans, and international banking services. Perhaps most importantly, Sparkassen can invest their surplus revenues with Landesbanken in the form of short-term deposits or bonds, thereby allowing Sparkassen to manage their maturity transformation risk, i.e., the risk of using short-term deposits to make long-term loans.

Eleven regional banking associations share ownership of Landesbanken and play an essential administrative role within the S-Group network. Regional associations are supported through fees levied on member Sparkassen. Regional associations service their savings bank members in many ways, including running data centres, lobbying state governments, developing new financial products, conducting marketing campaigns, doing economic and market research, and providing training, procurement, and auditing services. As a link between savings banks and Landesbanken, regional bank associations coordinate the activities within the network. Most importantly, state laws require that regional associations conduct annual audits of their member Sparkassen and monitor their business activities; the associations are thus the lynchpin in the oversight of Sparkassen. Finally, regional banking associations are governed by their members. Larger institutions contribute a larger share of the regional associations' budgets. However, governance of the regional association varies. In some cases the association relies on the principle of "one Sparkasse, one vote", which protects the interests of smaller savings banks within each region. Other associations allocate votes based on the size of a savings banks' capital stock ("*Stammkapital*") (Klein 2003: 201).

The third tier of the S-Group network operates at the national level and consists of the Deutsche Girozentrale known as DekaBank, Deutsche Leasing, and several investment and equity firms. DekaBank is the savings banks' investment company and offers savings banks and their customers the ability to participate in capital markets. With its subsidiaries, DekaBank forms the Deka Group, which holds nearly €100 billion in assets and is one of Germany's most significant investment providers and real estate management firms. The third tier also includes the DSGV, the national umbrella organization representing the S-Group, and co-owner of DekaBank. The DSGV represents the interests of the Sparkassen-Finanzgruppe on banking policy, regulatory law, and other banking industry issues on a national and international level. It also organizes decision-making and stipulates strategic direction within the group, acting in cooperation with the regional associations and other group institutions. The DSGV is supported financially by the regional associations and the Landesbanken.

Academic studies (Deeg 1999; Butzbach 2008), trade publications (Jankowski & Rickes 2018; Henneke 2019), news accounts, and interviews with Sparkassen managers, stakeholders, and competitors tout the importance of the network in strengthening and bolstering Germany's public savings banks. As one private banker put it bluntly, "Without the network Sparkassen would not exist". But how does this multi-tier network matter? How does being embedded within the S-Group affect Sparkassen's ability to compete? What advantages does the network give Sparkassen?

Economies of scale

The most immediate advantage the S-Group offers Sparkassen is economies of scale. Four areas referenced most often include branding/marketing, information technology (IT), training/human capital and regulatory compliance.

Regardless of where you go in Germany, the familiar red "S" is one of the most recognized symbols. Even though Sparkassen are primarily independent and autonomous credit institutions, they are identified by the public as part of a vast system of branches and banks. The regional associations and the DSGV promote the brand. In the 2019 *Readers Digest* study, 35 per cent of those surveyed listed Sparkassen as the most recognizable and trusted brand, a stark contrast to the two largest private banks, Commerzbank (6 per cent) and Deutsche Bank (3 per cent) (Lindenberg 2019).

IT is another area in which Sparkassen benefit from economies of scale. The S-Group established a subsidiary in Frankfurt, called Finanzinformatik, that developed a uniform IT system for the network including Sparkassen as early as 2008. The IT systems gave all savings banks, particularly the smaller ones, the ability to provide online banking services. A manager at a small credit institution, said, "Online banking is essential for our business, particularly to attract and maintain younger customers. But we could never have done online banking on our own. We lack the competence and the resources."

However, the real benefit of the IT system is that it establishes the back-end operations of the S-Group's banking services. Back-end operations are the backbone of any bank's infrastructure because it facilitates the integration of all the back-office parts of a credit institution including the applications that transmit prices, record historic data and execute orders to thousands of clients within milliseconds. The economies of scale that stem from the S-Group's IT system are particularly significant in that they benefit small and large institutions in analysing data, comparing institutions' performance and portfolios, and enabling all institutions to comply with and stay up-to-date with new and changing regulations. Data security and defence against money laundering, theft, and computer hacking are benefits that no single credit institution, regardless of size, could adequately manage or pay for.

Human capital development and training are another area where economies of scale matter. The 385 Sparkassen collectively constitute one of the largest employers in Germany, with 205,000 employees. The S-Group trains 15,000 interns each year, most of whom work in one of the local Sparkasse branches. The DSGV and regional banking associations teach large numbers of Sparkassen employees across every area of banking. The S-Group has its own university in Bonn, the University of Applied Science of the Savings Banks Finance Group, which offers Sparkassen employees and trainees the opportunity to obtain an internationally recognized academic degree in banking, finance, marketing and cooperation.[14] Also, each of the 11 regional savings bank associations run their own training academies.

According to respondents, the economies of scale applied to human resource development provide Sparkassen with three significant advantages. First, they spread the cost of training across the entire network and enable even the smallest Sparkassen to benefit. Second, they standardize the training and credentialism, making it easier for employees to move within the network. And finally, training socializes employees to values associated with public banking such as social responsibility, relational banking, transparent and effective oversight, and fiscal prudence. The socialization is particularly relevant to mid-level or top-tier managerial hires from private banks unfamiliar with the public mission of savings banks or the role supervisory boards (consisting of employee representatives) play in the governance of the bank. As one manager put it, even if an intern or young employee leaves the S-Group for a private bank, "their understanding of banking and finance will be influenced by the training they received within the S-Group". Each Sparkasse benefits directly from the investment in human capital made by the network.

Loan approval

Business lending is the core of the Sparkassen business model. Yet, smaller financial institutions often struggle to compete with larger institutions because large banks have more sophisticated loan approval systems. Sparkassen gain access to advanced loan approval systems because of their network. Sparkassen provide and receive customer lending data through an S-Group subsidiary. This is important for three reasons. First, it provides additional information to overcome the information asymmetry problems described in earlier chapters. Being able to tap into an extensive database of similar customers in similar industries improves relational banking by more efficiently pricing loans and risk. A CEO noted: "If you look in the whole country of Germany, then you have got millions of balance sheets which I can access and with this information ... you know if the pricing of a loan is right, but you also know how this company is behaving compared with the others". Moreover, savings banks can get this information efficiently and at relatively low cost because they are embedded in the network.

Second, access to regional data enables Sparkassen to provide advice and guidance to business customers about markets and competitors. One Sparkassen CEO referred to this as "branch analysis". It is something all banks do, but the S-Group network's dataset is particularly helpful. The S-Group subsidiary does the review, but it is employees at the local savings bank who convey the information to the customer about the industry, sector, and region and compare the numbers to the customer's business plan.

Finally, because they are independent entities, Sparkassen make decisions on loan approvals without the need to consult a central office outside the region. As discussed in Chapter 3, Sparkassen's primary business clients are SMEs who want to talk to a competent person at their local branch. Private banks deserted more impoverished regions of the country. And even where private bank branches exist, they often lack the authority to make loan decisions. Sparkassen's advantage derives from their local connection, independence and flexibility in the loan approval. As Schackmann-Fallis *et al.* (2017: 17) write, the network preserves, "the benefits of decentralized decision-making, client proximity, and local expertise ... This is particularly important in corporate banking with SMEs and craft enterprises".

Regulatory compliance

A further advantage for Sparkassen from being embedded in the S-Group is in the area of regulation. Sparkassen are required to comply with the same domestic regulations as any financial institution in Germany. Moreover, in the wake of the financial crisis, the scope and quantity of regulation have increased. Increased regulation is often cited as a factor that drives financial institutions to merge and reduces the ability of small banks to compete. The regulatory burden was mentioned as a significant challenge by every respondent interviewed for this book. However, Sparkassen enjoy an administrative advantage many other smaller institutions lack a network.

Because they are embedded within the S-Group network, smaller Sparkassen in particular can take advantage of assistance from the central and the regional banking associations. Sparkassen also help each other in complying with new regulations. For example, one CEO reported that in the state of Hessen, eight small Sparkassen (known as the eight *Zwerge* or gnomes) help each other with regulatory compliance, "they divide up the work in figuring out how to answer certain questions or complete certain forms". The network facilitates cooperation between savings banks because savings banks do not compete with each other, and collaboration offers them a competitive advantage over private banks and cooperatives.

Access to capital markets

Arguably the most important advantage the network offers Sparkassen is the ability to invest excess reserves and offer their customers access to capital markets. Excess reserves occur when a savings bank takes in more deposits than it can lend out to businesses or individuals. It presents a particular challenge both in a low-interest-rate environment in which banks struggle to earn returns on their assets that can match their deposit liabilities, and in regions of the country that struggle economically and where the supply of deposits exceeds the demand for investment and credit. Moody's Investor Service notes that Sparkassen's net interest-rate margin, the difference between interest-earning assets and interest-bearing liabilities, was stable until 2015 and then declined to put Sparkassen under increased pressure to find other sources of income (Moody's Investor Service 2018).

Sparkassen responded by increasing fees on current accounts (*Girokontos*), reducing the interest to depositors, selling investments to customers, and investing their reserves. The amount Sparkassen earn from fees and commissions versus credit has steadily increased over time. The S-Group creates a pathway through which Sparkassen and their customers have access to capital markets. DekaBank creates the financial products that are sold to the banks and by the banks to customers. The savings banks are free to sell any fund, but they typically sell Deka funds in part because of the close intra-network relationship between Sparkassen and DekaBank. As one DekaBank representative put it, "We understand Sparkassen and their appetite for risk. We are more likely to offer Sparkassen and their customers safe products rather than products with high returns. Our funds are about hedging against the downsides of the market rather than earning high profits. Sparkassen would have no understanding if we took an aggressive position in the capital market to achieve a high return."

Excess reserves are invested in DekaBank, the regional Landesbanken, or lent out to Sparkassen with a surplus of loans. The ability to invest reserves within the network is an essential advantage for Sparkassen, particularly those in poorer regions of the country. A Sparkassen CEO in eastern Germany reported that two-thirds of his funds were invested in bonds issued by his regional Landesbank or financial products from DekaBank, with only a third of his deposits lent out as credit to SMEs. Savings banks would prefer to loan out their deposits to regional customers. However, in poorer districts of the country, there are not enough borrowers. The CEO stated, "We have more deposits from customers than in the west and fewer credit. It's always growing apart. That's a big problem. We don't have any industry. We have only a couple of giant energy companies that are too big for us." The ability to invest in capital markets via the network is an important tool Sparkassen use to manage their risk, remain competitive, and maintain their resilience in a low-interest-rate environment.

Regulatory treatment of the network

The institutional protection scheme confers a significant regulatory advantage also enjoyed by cooperatives (Choulet 2017).[15] Under Article 113(7) of Europe's Capital Requirements Regulation (CRR), the S-Group and its members are treated as entities within a consolidated banking group such as Deutsche Bank or Citigroup. What this means is that members of the network, including Sparkassen, do not need to hold capital to cover risks from their exposure to other members of the same network. In other words, to determine how much reserve capital a Sparkassen must hold against their investments, the CRR treats the S-Group as a single holding company and exempts those investments made within the network from capital reserve requirements (European Central Bank 2016). This is a significant advantage since the majority of Sparkassen investments are in Landesbanken or DekaBank (Choulet 2017, 2019). At the same time, in assessing which financial institutions are "systemically important" under Europe's Single Supervisory Mechanism, the ECB treats the majority of Sparkassen as small banks not subject to direct scrutiny by the ECB. In short, under EU law, the network gives Sparkassen the regulatory advantages of a large banking holding company and the regulatory advantages of being a small "less significant" independent bank. Those regulatory advantages, coupled with the ability to invest reserves within the network, bolsters the competitiveness and resilience of Sparkassen, even in those regions that struggle economically.

In short, administration is an important reason for Sparkassen's ability to compete with larger private banks. The network within which Sparkassen are embedded give the small savings banks many comparative advantages. However, the network also establishes a unique set of formal and informal institutions that ensure Sparkassen stick to their "boring" business model (Schackmann-Fallis *et al.* 2017).

Administrative mechanisms of oversight and accountability

A mystery at the centre of Sparkassen's experience during the financial crisis is how they managed to stay the course despite domestic and global pressures. Landesbanken, the regional banks within the S-Group, failed to stick to their traditional business model and paid a heavy price (Gubitz 2013; Scherrer 2014; Cassell 2016). Much has been written about why private banks and regional public banks failed, and why regulators and regulatory frameworks failed to check their risky behaviour (Gubitz 2013; Schrooten 2009; Seikel 2013). Less is known about how public savings banks stuck to their cautious business model, avoided the mistakes made by their regional public partners and private competitors, maintained stable levels of profitability, kept administrative costs low, and fulfilled their public mandate.

Recall that, in addition to earning a profit, public savings banks are required by state laws to provide a set of public goods that include:

- serving the financial needs of all those who live and do business in the region (including refugees);
- maintaining credit for SMEs in the region;
- promoting savings, self-sufficiency and economic literacy;
- strengthening the region's economic competitiveness; and
- supporting civil society groups (Brämer *et al.* 2010).

Mixing public and private mandates, coupled with the sheer number of independent savings banks across a large region, creates accountability challenges. And yet, throughout the global financial crisis, savings banks earned steady and consistent profits, fulfilled their public mandates, and avoided the risky ventures that plagued larger public and private banks.

One administrative factor that accounts for Sparkassen's resilience is the Institutional Protection System (IPS) established in 1975. About half of eurozone credit institutions are members of an IPS, a form that is only recognized in Austria, Germany and Spain. In Germany, three out of four credit institutions are members of an IPS, including public banks and cooperatives. According to European regulations, an IPS is a "contractual or statutory liability arrangement which protects those institutions and in particular, ensures their liquidity and solvency to avoid bankruptcy where necessary" (Article 113(7) CRR) (Choulet 2017). An IPS combines two concepts: an "institutional guarantee" (*Institutssicherung*) that operates under a "joint-liability scheme" (*Haftungsverbund*). If a savings bank in the town of Erfurt runs into financial difficulty, the entire S-Group network, including the other 378 savings banks, guarantee the institution's solvency and protect creditors and depositors. Although the IPS behaves as a centralized entity, what is unusual is that the S-Group consists of independent and autonomous institutions, including 385 independent savings banks. The IPS effect on oversight is elucidated by contrasting it with a traditional government deposit insurance system like the United States' FDIC.

All deposit insurance systems require credit institutions to pay into a fund. The amount paid reflects the banks' total assets and risk profile. Larger and riskier banks pay more than smaller, less risky banks. Funds protect depositors and reduce the chance of a "run" on the bank. A bank run occurs when customers withdraw their deposits simultaneously over concern for the bank's solvency, triggering more people to withdraw funds, increasing the probability of default, and prompting even more deposit withdrawals. In short, bank liability insurance was created to protect the economy from financial panics. In most cases, deposit insurance systems are operated by a government.

A problem, however, is that insurance funds can create issues of moral hazard and adverse selection. Deposit insurance removes the motivation for depositors to withdraw funds from poorly-managed banks at risk of default, and undisciplined bankers lose the incentive to manage risks (Merton 1977). By capturing profits and shifting losses to a public entity, banks are incentivized to engage in risky behaviour while the incentive for depositors and shareholders to monitor banks' behaviour is lowered, thereby increasing the chance of insolvency and losses. Government-run deposit insurance systems thus require government regulators capable of accurately assessing the moral-hazard and selection-bias risks of a credit institution (Allen *et al.* 2012). The 2007/8 financial crisis and the Savings and Loan crisis in the late 1980s showed that when government regulators lack accurate information on the health of each institution, or cannot act quickly enough, the entire system is threatened (Pizzo *et al.* 1989; Johnson & Kwak 2011; Aliber & Kindleberger 2015). A public system also sets up an adversarial dynamic between a government that seeks accurate information and credit institutions who wish to reduce their regulatory burden (Konzelmann & Fovargue-Davies 2013; Moran 2010). In the lead-up to the S&L crisis of the 1980s and the 2007/08 financial crisis, credit institutions were notorious in keeping regulators in the dark about the riskiness of their assets. In the case of the opaque "over-the-counter" derivatives market, the US Congress prevented government regulators from collecting the information necessary to assess the systemic risk (Johnson & Kwak 2011; Das 2010). Effective oversight becomes a function of the political process, and the skill and willingness of legislators and regulators to override the concerns of clientele groups representing the financial sector (Calomiris 1990; Kane 1989; Cassell 2002).

Privately-run deposit insurance systems operate differently (Calomiris 1990). They work through a network of branches rather than a single "unit bank" (Powers 1969). A large geographic area reduces the vulnerability from an economic downturn in one particular region or industry. In private systems, banks agree to share liabilities, make interbank loans, and coordinate suspensions and resumptions of convertibility. Suspension of convertibility refers to when a bank, facing a run on deposits and needing to remain solvent, refuses to allow customers to withdraw deposits. Accountability in private deposit systems is a function of self-regulation and mutual monitoring. As joint liability holders, member banks have an incentive to oversee and collect information about each other's business and take proactive steps to ensure a member institution does not fail. Before the introduction of government deposit insurance in the United States in 1933, private schemes were common, particularly in agricultural states like Ohio, Indiana and Iowa (Morton 1943).

The S-Group's IPS uses a system of shared liability among its members to protect institutions, creditors and depositors. Credit institutions and depositors are protected through a private deposit insurance system embedded within a national and supranational system of regulation. Sparkassen are subject to the same federal banking regulations and bank regulatory framework as all private and public credit institutions in Germany.[16] National and European regulations constitute the primary oversight mechanism for all credit institutions in Germany, including Sparkassen. However, the joint liability scheme creates the most proximate sources of accountability and sets Sparkassen apart from private banks.

Before turning to how savings banks are kept in line, it is helpful to understand how the IPS system is set up. The S-Group's IPS consists of a set of tiered bank insurance funds that correspond to the structure of the S-Group network. The S-Group's IPS differs from other bank liability systems in that it insures the institution, including creditors (not just depositors). Creditors include regional banks and companies whose deposits provide additional source capital beyond deposits. The financing of the system works like other banks' insurance funds. First, each Sparkasse pays premiums into a mutual fund based on their total assets and risk profile. There are 11 savings bank guarantee funds governed by each of the 11 regional bank associations within which each savings bank is a member. Also, there is a separate insurance fund for all Landesbanken and for the regional building societies (Landesbausparkassen), which specialize in home loans for private households. Altogether there are 13 separate guarantee funds, each with their governing structure yet still part of the larger network.

The tiered liability funds mean every actor in the network is liable for the actions of all members of the network. This creates an incentive within the network to safeguard each Sparkasse, protect the Sparkassen brand, and preserve the trust of customers and the population at large. The insurance system protects customer deposits (as in the case of a government deposit insurance system). Still, it is designed to protect and preserve the institutions, thereby avoiding costly deposit payouts while retaining stable business relations.

While national regulators monitor regulatory compliance, Sparkassen's accountability system is focused on monitoring and identifying risks and vulnerabilities early to take proactive measures to reduce the chance of a bank failure. According to respondents, this requires (1) efficient, effective monitoring; (2) significant trust within the network; and (3) an organizational culture in which employees are socialized into a set of public and private values. The following discusses each factor in turn.

Risk monitoring

The central feature of the Sparkassen's accountability is a risk monitoring system. Each of the 1l regional funds oversees and monitors their member savings banks' risk. Drawing on quantitative data collected throughout the year, each fund's monitoring committee uses a "traffic light" system to rate a savings bank's risk. Green indicates no evidence of risk. Yellow indicates some evidence of increased risk. And red indicates significant evidence of a highly risky activity requiring intensive monitoring and potential action. Quantitative information used by the monitoring committee to make its assessment includes: profit and risk indicators, risk capacity assessment; capital ratios; and bank liquidity. Once a score is assigned, the monitoring committee prepares a qualitative report based on additional information from the bank's management and supervisory board. The qualitative report enables the monitoring committee to downgrade the bank from green to yellow or yellow to red. With each downgrade, the committee requests additional information, imposes greater external monitoring, and increases the banks' contribution to their bank association's insurance fund.

As part of the on-going risk-monitoring system, each savings bank is required by state law to undergo an external audit. Mandatory audits are common among all companies. However, most firms, including private banks and cooperatives, hire private accounting firms like KMPG or PricewaterhouseCoopers. Because a client selects the auditing firm, auditors may exhibit what economists call "unconscious bias" – overly positive assessments designed to keep clients happy (Brewster *et al.* 2019). Sparkassen also undergo annual audits. However, public savings banks have no choice over who does the review. State banking laws require that audits of savings banks be conducted by the auditing staff of the banking association in which the bank is a member. This reduces unconscious bias since auditors work for the larger network, which has a strong self-interest to protect the guaranteed funds. A former regulator with the Federal Financial Supervisory Authority made the point, "The audits conducted by the banking association examiners are extremely thorough without exception and the reason is simple: in contrast to their private counterparts, the public bank examiners do not have to worry that if they do their job well, they will be thrown out. We had Sparkassen examiners call us, the federal regulators, in cases where they thought a savings bank was operating outside the limits of their capacity." Referring to the auditing process, a Sparkassen CEO said simply that the system works because "we cannot cherry-pick the auditor we want". Examiner autonomy is further strengthened by two additional factors: the auditing section within each banking association enjoys its own independent budget, and auditors regularly rotate through different banks to ensure their evaluations are unbiased, transparent, and honest.

Trust

Trust is the lubricant that makes the system function smoothly. According to respondents, the risk-monitoring processes benefit from a high level of trust among stakeholders. The early-warning system requires constant monitoring and information flowing back and forth from the credit institution to their respective banking associations and funds. Trust facilitates those flows; it makes it more likely a bank will share problematic data, and more likely that the risk monitoring system will quickly identify unusually risky behaviour.

One reason for the trust is the closed – and private – nature of the process. Sensitive information is more easily shared and collected within the network precisely because it is outside the public eye. Audit information about a specific institution is closely guarded by the DSGV, regional associations, and the Bundesbank. While this frustrates journalists and researchers, the closed nature of the process helps maintain trust between banks and their respective association monitoring committees. Incorporating savings bank CEOs into the monitoring committees and risk-monitoring process also increases confidence.

Along with savings bank managers, monitoring committees include auditors, insurance fund managers, and the heads of the respective national or regional association. An additional factor that increases trust among network actors is a separate transparency committee within the network that oversees monitoring standards, reviews risk-adjusted contributions to the fund, and ensures due diligence is practiced (OECD 2014: 64). And finally, smaller banks make up the bulk of the network. One might expect them to feel overwhelmed or threatened by the interests of larger savings banks. Indeed several Sparkassen CEOs noted the tension between large and small institutions over issues of oversight and accountability. However, trust in the risk monitoring processes is maintained because in most regional associations, each bank (regardless of size or contribution to the association) is given one vote in the governance of their association.

Socialization

Finally, socialization within the S-Group is an essential organizational feature of oversight and accountability that complements the more formal risk-monitoring system. Sparkassen employees share a set of norms and values that combine elements of the public and private sectors. Once an arm of local governments, Sparkassen retain classical elements of bureaucratic organizations, including clear lines of authority, strict adherence to rules and procedures, commitment to public service and public sector ethics, a standard pay-grade system applied across the network, and a transparent certification and promotion system. At the same time, Sparkassen are for-profit universal banks competing with private and co-operative credit institutions. And the S-Group overall competes globally to offer every type of domestic and international financial product and service. Sparkassen employees are thus trained in every aspect of banking, real estate and finance.

In 2019 the S-Group employed 15,000 apprentices. It is common for individuals, once hired, to spend their entire career within the S-Group moving laterally across Sparkassen and horizontally between the different firms within the S-Group. Every savings bank CEO respondent interviewed for this book started their career in an entry-level position in a savings bank. As one employee representative at the DSGV put it, "Not all who start their careers in the S-Group remain. Yet, even those who leave take with them values that set them apart from their private banking colleagues."

In contrast, careers in the private financial sector are characterized as "churn and burn" (Ufer 2017; Quinlan 2017). Short-term employment is the norm, the environment is hyper-competitive, and new hires often assume they must leave the firm after only a couple of years to rise through the ranks. A PricewaterhouseCooper survey of the financial sector found that only 10 per cent of millennials working for private financial firms planned to stay for the long term, and half said they were already looking for a new position elsewhere (PricewaterhouseCoopers 2012). And a LinkedIn study of 12 global investment banks found that analysts who left their positions in 2015 held their job for an average of 17 months (Quinlan 2017).

The tenure of S-Group employees socialized into a set of public/private norms helps to keep savings banks from straying too far from their "boring bank" business model. As independent credit institutions, Sparkassen managers enjoy discretion in how they run their institutions. Sparkassen CEOs interviewed acknowledged that it is legally possible for their banks to take unreasonable risks. However, the values shared by employees within the organization keep banks in check. Moreover, close relations within the network also mean that anomalous risky behaviour by any one bank is quickly discovered. CEOs and other top Sparkassen managers acknowledge the importance of peer pressure within the S-Group. There is a strong sense of community among Sparkassen managers in large part because most have spent their careers within the S-Group and because of the incentives within the IPS. Regional banking associations and the DSGV hold regular conferences and workshops attended by managers, staff and supervisory board members. Savings bank CEOs sit on committees together, they consult with each other, and they work together on business deals. And their tenure within the S-Group means managers experience the consequences of their decisions. Finally, while savings banks do not compete with each other, "No savings bank wants to look bad in front of the others. We know each other, and we make sure that our colleagues are not investing in areas they know nothing about."

In short, the IPS protects savers, institutions, and the public in several ways. First, geography matters. Spreading risk across a large geographic region like Germany protects banks in the network against a financial panic stemming from economic decline in one region or a single industry. In addition, by insuring creditors (rather than just depositors), the bank insurance system institutionally supports the network of banking relationships upon which the Sparkassen business model depends (Deeg & Donnelly 2016) and further stabilizes regions.

Second, treating 385 savings banks as independent credit holds each savings bank (and its supervisory board) responsible for fulfilling the public mandates specified in state savings bank laws. Local leaders with an incentive to ensure Sparkassen pursue the public goals in their region are authorized to oversee their bank's actions. Decentralization reduces the chance of banks profiting from the risks taken by another bank, thus reducing moral hazard problems. Moreover, supervisory board members (selected by local government sponsors and employee representatives), those most familiar with the banks' activities, are empowered to oversee the banks' actions, thereby reducing problems of information asymmetry (Noack 2009).

Third the IPS protects savers because oversight is conducted by the network itself rather than a state agency. It is an example of a "private interest government" and a characteristic of Germany's system of ordoliberalism (Streeck & Schmitter 1985). Joint liability within the network creates incentives to hold banks accountable proactively. Problems are detected early on because of the steady flow of information, and because regional bank associations use their database of savings bank information to compare the activities of any one bank. As a member of a monitoring committee noted, "We can quickly see if a savings bank takes on an unusual amount of risk because we are constantly looking at all institutions in the region. Unusual activity stands out." Bank examiners within each banking association also develop the expertise to monitor banking activity in their particular region. This is important because savings banks' clients differ throughout the country. To effectively oversee the operations of a savings bank in Hanover or Heilbronn, for example, means understanding the industries particular to those regions. The network structure enables that type of specialization to occur.

In short, administration is an essential piece of the puzzle in explaining why Sparkassen survived and thrived during the past two decades, and why they remain so resilient. Global competition, increased regulations, and low interest rates would usually favour large private institutions with enormous economies of scale and business models centred on fees and commissions rather than lending to SMEs and individuals. Moreover, one might expect small independent public savings banks overseen by government representatives with little experience in high finance to be particularly susceptible to promises of high returns from risky opaque financial products. Yet, Sparkassen largely resisted such temptations and stuck to their boring business banking model.

Administration contributed to their resilience in two essential ways. First, Sparkassen's place within a large network provides the credit institutions with a number of advantages that allow the small independent institutions to compete effectively with larger private competitors. In a sense, administration allows Sparkassen to enjoy the benefits of being small, local, and directly connected to a loyal customer base. At the same time, administration also enables Sparkassen to reap the advantages of being part of one of the largest financial networks in the world. And second, the administrative structure that insures institutions, creditors, and depositors within the S-Group explains how Sparkassen have primarily stayed the course during the past two decades despite pressures to take on higher risk. The IPS is not the primary regulator of Germany's savings banks: the Bundesbank and the Federal Financial Supervisory Authority are. The IPS creates a set of formal (insurance fund and risk monitoring systems) and informal (trust and socialization) structures that keep Sparkassen from straying from their core lending business model. In other words, the IPS maintains a set of intra-network incentives, relationships, and capacities to ensure banks fulfill their public mandate obligations and act proactively to reduce the chance of a savings bank taking on unusual risk.

6

POLITICAL EXPLANATIONS

"We have a lot of influence, of course ... whoever has the money has the power. That's the way it is. But you won't see us in the paper every day. Our influence is indirect, through our presence in the region and the community. Our people are everywhere." – Sparkassen CEO

One of the mysteries of Germany's public savings banks is how they manage to navigate domestic and global forces that brought down similar credit institutions in other countries. Public institutions generally and public banks in particular, have been under attack since the 1980s when conservative governments passed a wave of neoliberal reforms (Brown 2015; Scherrer 2017). Public savings banks across European countries – Italy, Spain, Britain, France – disappeared, consolidated, or transformed into private entities that are mostly indistinguishable from private banks. In most cases, domestic legislation changed the banking landscape in ways that undermined public savings banks' business model. In France, for example, a 1999 law transformed savings banks into a legal form of private cooperative banks (Polster 2005). In Italy, a series of reforms in the 1990s privatized public banks and eliminated their regional requirements (Carletti *et al.* 2005). And in Spain, legislation in the 1980s and 1990s led to partial privatization and the elimination of the regional principle.

In Germany, private bank leaders make little secret of their feelings toward public savings banks. It is a mixture of envy and contempt (Schulz 2010). When respondents from private banks including the Bundesverband der deutschen Banken (BdB), the trade association that represents private banks, were asked what enables Sparkassen to be successful, they offered the following list of grievances: 1) Sparkassen control the retail banking market and make it difficult for private banks to compete, "They are in every city and county. The cost of entering those markets is enormous"; 2) their public identity gives Sparkassen an unfair advantage, "They're operating at a loss in a number of places. A private bank couldn't do that"; 3) the S-Group network enables Sparkassen to be both small and local, and large and national at the same time, "They wouldn't stand a chance on their own"; and 4) their institutional protection scheme gives Sparkassen an unfair regulatory advantage in complying with the Capital Regulatory Directive (CRD). However, what is most frustrating to the private bank respondents is the Sparkassen's success in branding. One respondent compared the public banks to Telekom, Germany's notoriously inefficient public telecommunications firm: "Sparkassen charge higher fees and pay less interest. Nevertheless, people still use them. Why? Because they know them, especially the elderly. It's like the Telekom. I will never understand why people are willing to pay more for the exact same services." Germany's private banks have tried to pass legislation with little success that would end the regional principle and allow Sparkassen to be sold or privatized (Donges *et al.* 2001; Köhler 2004).

At the European level, the pressure against Sparkassen is even greater. In addition to ending state guarantees, the European Commission has pushed European banking union, policies that seek to establish a single banking supervisor, a single set of rules to regulate and resolve institutions, and a single system to protect depositors. Such changes undermine advantages small regional institutions like Sparkassen and credit unions enjoy by, for example, replacing their IPS with a European-wide Deposit Insurance Scheme. So far, European banking union remains incomplete thanks in large part to the efforts of Germany's Sparkassen and credit unions.

So how have Sparkassen managed to fend off hostile legislation and public policies even as public savings banks in other countries have failed? The answer is power. An important reason for Sparkassen's resilience is their ability to defend themselves politically. Popular press accounts often exaggerate Sparkassen's political influence, particularly at the EU level. Magazines and newspapers rely on hyperbole and caricatures when they discuss public savings banks. *Die Zeit*, a German national newspaper, for example, described savings banks as the most powerful group in Berlin (Schieritz & Storn 2012). The newspaper described Georg Fahrenschon, the former head of the DSGV, as the most powerful lobbyist in Germany, well ahead of the president of Deutsche Bank. Moreover, *Der Spiegel Online* describes Sparkassen as the most influential lobby group in all of Germany (Hesse *et al.* 2012). And the *Wall Street Journal* went even further, claiming Sparkassen to be among the most powerful political players in the world (Stevens & Steinauser 2013). The German public is highly critical of lobbying, and such accounts often deliberately paint a distorted picture of Sparkassen and the DSGV as powerful actors operating behind the scenes to undermine the European Union. Such accounts are incorrect, misleading and overly-simplistic.

A quick scan of the data on EU lobbying reveals that the DSGV's investment in lobbying the European Union pales in comparison to the resources that private and commercial banks devote to shaping EU financial regulations and banking union. LobbyFacts, a non-profit that tracks lobbying of European institutions, notes the DSGV spent €1.8 million on lobbying in Brussels in 2018. By contrast, private banks represented by dozens of organizations spent 20 to 30 times more on buying political influence than the DSGV (see Table 6.1). The DSGV ranks 118 among registered lobbyists and within the hierarchy of financial industry lobbying, the DSGV is near the bottom.

Table 6.1 Comparison of EU lobbying by financial firm, 2018

Overall rank	Lobby organization	Country	Lobbying expenditures
11	Insurance Europe	Belgium	€6,500,000–6,749,000
20	Association for Financial Markets in Europe	United Kingdom	€4,500,000–4,749,000
21	European Banking Federation	Belgium	€4,500,000–4,749,000
34	European Fund and Asset Management Association	Belgium	€3,500,000–3,749,000
51	Bundesverband Öffentlicher Banken Deutschlands	Germany	€2,750,000–2,999,999
58	BVI Bundesverband Investment und Asset Management e.V.	Germany	€2,500,000–2,749,000
81	Deutsche Bank AG	Germany	€2,270,000
85	Bundesverband deutscher Banken e.V.	Germany	€2,000,000–2,249,999
92	International Swaps and Derivatives Association	United States	€2,000,000–2,249,999
97	Associazione Bancaria Italiana	Italy	€1,750,000–1,999,999
118	Deutscher Sparkassen- und Giroverband (DSGV)	Germany	€1,800,000
123	Bundesverband der Deutschen Volksbanken und Raiffeisenbanken	Germany	€1,500,000–1,749,000

Source: Lobbyfacts.eu

In short, popular claims of the DSGV's influence are wildly overstated. In terms of sheer resources and staff, lobby groups representing private banks and credit institutions far exceed those of Sparkassen, credit unions or public banks. Indeed, the figures underestimate the power of groups opposed to public banks because the list omits business organizations and other industries hostile toward public banks. The data also leave out the close relationship between

EU lawmakers, Commission bureaucrats and private banks. In one of the more egregious "revolving door" examples in 2020, Adam Farkas, executive director of the EBA, became the chief executive of the Association for Financial Markets in Europe, a lobbying group representing the largest private banks in the world (Fleming & Brunsden 2020)

The real story is that Sparkassen have managed to defend themselves despite the enormous opposition to public banks particularly outside of Germany and the disadvantage in lobbying resources. However, merely claiming Sparkassen have power and influence, as media accounts often do, is insufficient to explain their success and resilience. The story is more nuanced, more complicated, and more interesting.

Public savings banks exercise power in a variety of ways. In some cases, public savings banks are direct, for example, in their lobbying effort against EDIS. In other ways, Sparkassen's influence is subtle and indirect, for example, shaping the public's views through involvement in civil society groups. Moreover, as Germany is a federalist system embedded within Europe, Sparkassen are effective in part because they exercise their power and influence differently at different levels of government. What is remarkable is not that Sparkassen are powerful but that Germany's public savings banks have succeeded despite the odds. This chapter explains how they've done it.

The first section draws on sociological and political theories of power to appreciate how Sparkassen exercise their influence. The following section then turns to how savings banks exercise power at the local level, the level of government where Sparkassen are the centre of economic life. Attention is paid to the sources of local power and draws on an example of Sparkassen's power in action – the decision of paying out dividends to local government sponsors – to illustrate how the banks exercise their influence. The final section examines how Sparkassen exercise power nationally and at the European level. Particular attention is paid to how Sparkassen maintain and reproduce their influence at the national and supranational level and then considers Sparkassen's role in shaping legislation to establish a European Banking Union (EBU) including a European Deposit Insurance Scheme (EDIS). There are a variety of ways one can study Sparkassen's power. The levels of government and the two examples offer a clear and unfettered view of the complexity of Sparkassen's ability to defend themselves and promote their interests. Drawing on interviews and other sources of data from the field, the chapter offers a descriptive exploration of Sparkassen's power. The puzzle explored is what does that power look like? Where does the power come from? Furthermore, how does that power and influence shield Germany's savings banks from policies that brought down similar banks in other countries?

What does political power mean?

There is a robust literature in political economy on the power and influence in Germany's public banking sector. The bulk of the work relies on a principal–agent framework to understand the impact political actors have on public banks' behaviour and performance (Lane 2006). This scholarship often assumes that policymakers seek to manage or influence public banks for political or electoral advantage (Göbel 2015). Deo *et al.* (2015), for example, find lawmakers are reluctant to close banks in their jurisdiction, and national politicians support those banks that are important for their governing coalition. Similarly, Behn and Haselmann (2016) find that the decision to recapitalize a struggling public bank is affected by local and state elections. Jonas Markgraf's work (2018), in particular, finds that politicians use Sparkassen for political ends by influencing the lending behaviour of banks.

Yet other work reverses the equation while still maintaining the principal–agent framework. This work centres on the lack of expertise among politically-appointed supervisory board members. Sparkassen managers and CEOs take advantage of incompetent politically-appointed overseers, making decisions in the interest of the bank and bank management but not in the public's interest (Kunz 2018; Sackmann 2018). One widely-cited example of this work is Hau and Thum's (2009) study of supervisory boards on Germany's Landesbanken. Hau & Thum compared the qualifications of supervisory board members of Landesbanken with board members in private banks. Landesbanken supervisory members were less likely than the boards of private banks to have backgrounds in areas of banking-related competency such as business administration and accounting. Hau and Thum argue that this difference in backgrounds explains the poor performance of the Landesbanken.

These works share a view of power aimed at the relationship between the most proximate political principals and their organizational agents. Such principal/agent studies are important. However, the theoretical approach misses systemic sources of power linked to the institutional architecture within which Sparkassen are embedded. Sparkassen's ability, for example, to keep European-wide deposit insurance from being implemented is less a function of incompetent supervisory board members or clever bank CEOs, than the connective tissue that links each of the country's 385 local savings banks horizontally and vertically. It is that extensive network that fuels an institutional juggernaut few politicians within or outside of Germany seek to challenge. Nor does the principal–agent framework explain how Sparkassen successfully keep at bay legislative efforts to undermine their regional principle or compel Sparkassen to pay out dividends; or why customers continue to trust and use Sparkassen even as the public savings banks cut interest rates and rely more and more on fees. However, how should one think about power beyond a principal–agent framework?

Steven Lukes' seminal work, *Power: A Radical View*, describes three dimensions of power. The one-dimensional approach reflects the principal–agent assumptions by Markgraf, Hau and Thum, as well as pluralists like Nelson Polsby (1980) or Robert Dahl (2005). Power in this dimension is one actor forcing another actor to do something she does not want to do. Grievances are clear. Contestation is open to all parties and observable. Moreover, the source of power is primarily political resources – votes, jobs or influence – that can be brought to the political bargain. Power in the first dimension is exercised within the formal political arena for all to see.

Table 6.2 Three faces of political power

	One-dimensional	*Two-dimensional*	*Three-dimensional*
Proponents	Dahl, Polsby	Bachrach & Baratz, Schattschneider	Lukes, Gaventa, Edelman
Conception of power	Power as decision-making and lobbying	Power as decision-making, lobbying and agenda-setting	Power as decision-making, agenda-setting and preference-shaping
Focus of analysis	Formal political arena	Formal political arena and the informal process surrounding it (the "corridors of power")	Civil society more generally, especially the public sphere in which preferences are shaped
Methodological approach	"Counting" votes and decisions in decision-making arena	Ethnography of the corridors of power	Ideology critique – to demonstrate how actors misperceive their own material interests
Nature of power	Visible, transparent and measurable	Invisible and visible to agenda setters	Largely invisible – power distorts perceptions and shapes preferences.

Source: Hay (2002: 180).

For example, because of their power on supervisory boards local politicians, Markgraf and others argue, use "their" Sparkasse to pursue their electoral goals by ensuring loans are made on terms that are more advantageous to the borrower (voter) than would be the case without the electoral connection. The power politicians exercise in this case is transparent and visible, and the methodology used to measure power, in this case, can include votes, loans and decisions.

The second dimension of power is one in which power is exercised not through bargaining but exclusion (Schattscheider 1960; Bachrach & Baratz 1962). This "second face of power" occurs when an actor succeeds in compelling another actor to do something she does not want to do, yet there is no open contestation or political battle. Power may be exercised in the formal political arena or through an informal process surrounding the area. Old-boys' networks or informal relations may prevent issues from arising, aggrieved actors are prevented from participating in the political process, and controversial information which might generate public concern is kept from public view. Inaction or a lack of political bargaining is not a sign of approval, but a reflection of stilted and disjointed information flows, and barriers to participation. Since there are often non-decisions involved, ethnographies or case studies are often applied to identify where a second dimension of power exists and how it is applied. The sources of such power include the ability to set the agenda, establish the "rules of the game", or control the flow of information. These tools facilitate and maintain what Bachrach and Baratz term the "mobilization of bias".

Finally, the third dimension of power reflects the social construction of how we make sense of the world (Lukes 2004; Gaventa 1982). In this "third face power", one actor convinces another to do something that benefits the former yet may or may not be in the latter's best interest. This third dimension is arguably the most powerful because once a consensus over ideology emerges, it leads to outcomes that are self-fulfilling and self-reinforcing. One no longer needs to compel people to follow a direction; they do it enthusiastically on their own. Murray Edelman describes the third face of power as exercised through a process of socialization, control of information, and the creation of myths and symbols (Edelman 1985).

Sparkassen employ each dimension of power to maintain their place in Germany's political economy. However, interviews and other sources of data reveal that Sparkassen exercise power differently at different levels of government. Even though they are fundamentally local credit institutions with local government sponsors/owners, Sparkassen's influence extends to the national and supranational levels. The following section explores how Sparkassen exercise influence at different levels of government and, drawing on interviews and examples, consider how public savings banks rely on different "faces" of power to protect themselves but also how the banks develop and maintain their power.

Power at the local level

Sparkassen exercise considerable influence within their local communities. A supervisory board member described Sparkassen's influence by comparing it to other local institutions: "Visit nearly any small and medium-size town in

Germany, you'll see three buildings: city hall, a church, and a building with giant red S with a dot over it. All three are equally important. Our Sparkasse funds our community." According to respondents, Sparkassen's influence stems from several sources.

First, information asymmetries give the management board a significant advantage over the supervisory board. The supervisory board relies on bank management for information about the bank's business activities. Bank managers note that it was rare for a supervisory board to question management's recommendations for several reasons. First, the view shared by all respondents that savings banks are for-profit institutions whose hiring and business practices should be free of politics. Even private competitors of Sparkassen, cooperatives, and private banks, who are critical of savings banks, responded that Sparkassen must operate as private entities, according to market principles, and without political interference. In this sense, a contrast is drawn between Sparkassen and the 16 state development banks and the national Kreditanstalt für Wiederaufbau (KfW). Development banks' mission is to address market failures and promote economic development rather than pursue profit. As such, politicians play more of a role in the business practices and hiring decisions of development banks than they do with Sparkassen, where politicians are expected to keep arm's-length from the business decisions.

Also, Sparkassen supervisory boards only meet four times a year. They are thus very much part-time boards that rely on bank managers for support and information. One CEO also cited turnover among political representatives on the supervisory board as a common challenge. In addition, a third of the supervisory board are employee representatives who often share management's view of bank policy.

Supervisory boards are not without power. Board membership is a paid position, and the boards select the banks' CEO and management team, weighs in on strategic and capital plans, and is briefed at the end of the year on the financial health of the bank. However, several bank CEOs described the process of "socializing" or "teaching" new political representatives about how the bank works and its importance to the local community. CEOs are also quick to reference the number of bank employees/voters, good-paying jobs, and the sizeable tax bill paid by the bank. As a result, bank CEOs suggested that although they review a bank's performance and hire its management, the supervisory board typically defers to management on business-related issues. To use Lukes' typology, the boards' asymmetric relationship enables bank management to exercise all three faces of power vis-à-vis the local politicians on the supervisory board.

The banks' influence is bolstered further by being the primary source of capital for SMEs and individuals in the community. As discussed in Chapter 4, Sparkassen are the most critical and consistent sources of finance to firms in a community, particularly in less-populated and economically-weaker regions of the country. However, as one CEO put it, Sparkassen are politically relevant not because of their financing per se but because their financing places them at the centre of the community's economic life. "We literally are the anchor in the region", said one CEO. The banks, by design, have a substantial stake in the health and welfare of the communities in which they are located. As a result, Sparkassen managers sit on the boards of the most significant firms and civic institutions in the area. One CEO listed several high-profile boards he and his management team serve on, including the boards of the local hospital, building society and professional soccer club. Close relationships with local governments, businesses and community groups provide Sparkassen with important information about the economic health of the community. At the same time, being at the centre of economic life enables Sparkassen to shape how citizens and policymakers view the banks and create opportunities to influence the platforms and policies of political parties without being overtly partisan. As one bank manager put it, "We influence fundamentally the political, social, cultural and athletic life of the city, but we do not get involved in party politics".

Sparkassen's integration into civil society is fortified further through the financial sponsorship of and donations to local civic organizations and associations, school activities, museums and culture, and sporting activities. This type of charity is known as "*sponsoring*" and "*spenden*" and the DSGV reports that in 2017 that S-Group organizations (mainly Sparkassen) gave €447 million to social, cultural and athletic organizations. Sparkassen view sponsoring as a core component of their public mission. As a CEO put it, "It's how we fulfill our social obligation. If it's not for a social purpose we don't fund it." Public savings banks' annual reports prominently feature examples of sponsored groups and initiatives. Of course, it is common for credit institutions to give to charitable causes. What sets Sparkassen apart, however, is the breadth of their giving. In 2017, for example, the midsize Spree-Neisse Sparkasse located in Cottbus (population 100,000), on the Polish/German border, spent €2 million sponsoring over 600 projects and initiatives in the community. In the same year, the Sparkasse Oberhessen headquartered in the small town of Friedberg spent €670,000 on 1,115 projects and initiatives.

Although they advertise their sponsoring in annual reports and press releases, Sparkassen do not disclose systematic data on who receives support or the amount of support. Research by the newspaper, *Frankfurter Allgemeine Zeitung* and a non-profit research centre dedicated to investigative journalism, *Correctiv*, reported in 2016 that, "Most Sparkassen treat their sponsoring as if it were a state secret. Until today there has not been a single Sparkasse in Germany that has made available a complete list of grantees and amounts" (Sachse & Weigner 2016). The newspaper/think tank collaborative collected data from 32 Sparkassen for 2013 and 2014. What is surprising is the variety of groups supported by the banks: men's choir groups, history clubs, carnival clubs, shooting clubs, school groups, and associations that work with refugees. The amounts are typically less than €3,000, and the records reveal that recipients reflect every demographic in the community. Although sponsoring is a part of Sparkassen's public mission, sponsoring offers banks significant political advantages. It enables the savings banks to control how banks support their community. Each bank decides on its own, who receives financial support and how much. In one case, a bank CEO stated that his bank's giving strategy was to make sure every organization in every political jurisdiction receives something. Donations to a local hunting club, swimming club, school, film festival, theatre, or Christmas festival allow the savings bank to show its presence across all demographics within the local community. Sparkassen websites include easy to download Sparkassen logos in different sizes, which grant recipients are encouraged to include in their literature. The amounts are typically small, but the breadth of sponsorship is a necessary form of branding, one that reinforces the connection between the savings banks and the local communities. In that sense sponsoring is a tool for exercising a third face of power, shaping the public's views toward Sparkassen. At the same time, by controlling the sponsorship process and the information disclosed about who receives support, Sparkassen also exercise what Lukes terms a second face of power.

However, how does the power work? How is it exercised? Where does one observe Sparkassen's local power and influence in ways that sustain and defend the Sparkassen business model? One clear example of how Sparkassen's influence matters is in the case of dividends, known in German as *Ausschütungen*.

Battle of dividends

One of the features that distinguish public savings banks from private commercial banks and cooperatives is the disbursal of dividends. Shareholders in private credit institutions expect to receive a share of the business's profits in the form of a dividend. In the case of cooperatives, members expect a dividend if their bank does well. A feature of Germany's public savings banks is that while governments might use the banks in the same way individuals and firms use them, shareholders do not capitalize the banks in the same way private owners might capitalize a private bank (Köhler 2016). Instead, Sparkassen must build up their capital through the retention of profits. As a result, there are strict rules that govern how savings banks' annual profits can be used and the conditions under which they can pay out dividends to their local government sponsors/owners. Savings Bank Acts in each of Germany's 16 federal states govern the distribution of profits. Under these Acts, savings banks are only eligible to distribute profits if their capital reserves exceed a minimum level prescribed in the Acts. If savings banks meet the reserve requirement they may distribute the net profit on a percentage scale, depending on their level of capital. Weaker savings banks that are poorly capitalized *may* distribute fewer profits to the shareholders than stronger institutions. The rules ensure that only those savings banks that hold a sufficient level of capital can distribute profits. The operative word is "may" since Savings Bank Acts' dividends are permissive, not mandatory; the legislation does not require a bank to pay out dividends regardless of how profitable or successful the institution. For example, the state of Hessen's Savings Bank Act requires banks to maintain a specific capital reserve level. However, after the reserve is achieved: "Insofar as the remaining amount is not required to strengthen the reserves further, a measured portion of the remaining reserves *may* be paid out to the local government sponsors/owners" (§16 SpkG Hessisches Sparkassengesetz).[17] The laws make clear that dividends are possible but also that public savings banks are independent credit institutions empowered to decide for themselves whether and how much they will pay out. Interestingly, it is the supervisory boards that are authorized by law to decide on the dividends.

Notwithstanding state laws' permissive policies, the DSGV, regional associations, and most managers in the Sparkassen interviewed regard dividends as a threat to savings banks' independence and business model. A bank manager captured the tension: "This is always a struggle between shareholders saying: 'we would like to have some distribution of the profit', whereas the Sparkasse says 'we need some strength in order to do some lending, to do also some regional benefit'". One CEO of a medium-size Sparkasse expressed the perspective voiced by three out of the four CEOs interviewed:

> If you paid out dividends, the politicians would want some every year. They would come to expect it. Right now we're doing well, but what would happen if we were doing poorly? They would still expect the dividends. The bank has to remain strong. That's the most important. And paying out dividends undermines our core mission by reducing our capital.

The CEO's statement reflects several concerns expressed by most Sparkassen respondents. One concern is that dividends undermine the competitiveness of Sparkassen by reducing capital reserves and weakening Sparkassen's ability to withstand economic shocks. One CEO said forcefully, "We have to remain strong. We have capital reserves of 18 per cent. We are the capital-strongest savings bank in all of Germany. Yet we are not going to pay out dividends. Paying out dividends weakens us." A representative from the regional Sparkassen association from Hessen-Thüringen offered a more nuanced explanation during a 2019 television interview. Matthias Haupt, from the association, explained that threats from a global trade war and an unplanned Brexit require Sparkassen to build up a capital cushion to absorb potential economic shocks (Mayer 2019).

A second concern is that dividends come at the expense of sponsoring. A Sparkasse that pays out dividends to local governments reduces the funds available to sponsor local organizations. This is problematic because while Sparkassen control who is sponsored and with how much, city and county politicians have the final say in deciding how dividends are spent. Sparkassen would lose control over an essential source of local influence. A final concern, expressed by Sparkasse managers is that once a bank pays out a dividend, local governments will expect a payout every year. Another manager expressed concern over what happens to the dividends, "It goes to the municipality, in the normal budget and you can understand what happens: puff! – it goes off, nothing happens in particular."

Although most Sparkassen and their regional and national associations view dividends as irresponsible and imprudent, the view is not uniformly shared. One medium-sized public savings bank in the east pays out dividends annually as well as sponsors a significant number of civil society groups. The CEO acknowledged that within the S-Group he is an outlier; he views capital reserves as necessary, but they should not be a barrier to dividends. He explained his view on dividends:

> When you are successful like we are, I think it is smart to share the success a little. And it is also a part of our identification with local political leaders. They can say, 'Man, we have an amazing Sparkasse!' And twice a year I and the local political leaders make a contribution to our governing institutions. It's part of the story we tell: We are a regional institution. We earn our money here. And when we do well, we give back to the community. That's the story we tell. And it's good for us.

Other voices express a similar justification for dividends. Hessen's state auditor said in 2019, "If it is going well for the Sparkassen and it is going poorly for the local government, then the Sparkassen must show solidarity and share some of its profits" (Mayer 2019). Academics and local government officials throughout Germany also call on Sparkassen to pay dividends (Sachse 2016), particularly in jurisdictions with significant infrastructure needs and municipal debt. In one high-profile case, Düsseldorf's mayor sued the city's public savings bank and demanded a larger dividend. In 2014 the bank earned €104 million and paid out €3.3 million to the city ("Entscheidung der Aufsicht" 2016). The mayor ultimately forced the bank to pay out €25 million. So how common are Sparkassen dividends?

As with sponsoring, Sparkassen and their associations do not disclose systematic information about which banks pay out dividends or the amounts. However, several studies find that Sparkassen are effective at limiting the amount of dividends they pay out. In 2017 in Hessen, researchers found that 14 of the state's

33 savings banks paid €32 million in dividends to their government owners/sponsors. This was viewed by the state's auditor as a small amount given that the banks had earned €229 million the year before.

One of the few comprehensive studies by Germany's Bundesbank found that in 2012 most savings banks, 398 out of 418, had reserves that exceeded the threshold requirement and could, therefore, pay out a dividend to their shareholders. The researchers found that most savings banks (nearly two-thirds) did not pay out any dividends even though they could, and supervisory board members could insist that they do. Furthermore, the researchers found that in Germany's wealthiest states, Bavaria and Baden-Württemberg, for example, savings banks are the least likely to pay dividends. Whereas in some of the poorest regions, particularly in former-East Germany, savings banks are more likely to pay out dividends. More recent data suggests that numbers are even more extreme today. An even higher percentage of Sparkassen exceed the reserve threshold than in 2012, and an even lower number pay out dividends (Atzler 2016).

A study published in *Frankfurter Allgemeine Zeitung* found that in 2014, Sparkassen earned profits of more than €1.9 billion and paid out 14 per cent in dividends to local governments. Public savings banks in several large regions, including Köln, Munich, and Ulm earned respectively €27.4 million, €22.5 million and €21.6 million in profits yet paid no dividends to their local governments (Sachse 2016).

The results are particularly surprising given that it is Sparkassen supervisory boards, run by local political leaders, that decide whether to pay out a dividend and how much; and local governments in Germany struggle with debt and infrastructure needs. The Bertelsmann Stiftung's annual finance report on Germany's local governments found in 2018 that local governments and their associations had close to €130 billion of debt or about €1,500 per resident (Bertelsman Stiftung 2019).

The view that dividends undermine Sparkassen's ability to survive an economic crisis turned out to be prescient in 2020. Excess reserves not only enabled the savings banks to withstand the Great Recession, they played a central role in the banks' resilience in the wake of the Covid-19 recession. Indeed, it is because of their high capital reserves that Sparkassen continue to lend to SMEs even as some worried the recession might lead to a credit crunch.

What accounts for the fact that most Sparkassen pay no dividends and that Düsseldorf is the outlier? It is difficult to assess the claim that dividends are a threat to Sparkassen. It is likely the case that if all Sparkasse were suddenly expected to pay out dividends, the change would alter the public banks' business model by decreasing their control over revenues and cutting their ability to raise capital (Schreiber 2020; Drost, 2020). Yet the question remains: how do Sparkassen keep from paying out dividends?

One common explanation relates to the second and third faces of power argument. Several respondents suggested that many supervisory board members, particularly in the smaller savings banks, are unaware that dividends are even an option. Sparkassen CEOs and bank managers do not raise the topic of dividends ("I never bring up the topic of dividends. That would be ridiculous", said one CEO), and supervisory board members often do not ask. Instead, if the bank earns significant revenues, the focus is on sponsoring and the Sparkassen's role in the community. Other respondents acknowledged that new supervisory board members sometimes call for dividends, but as one CEO pointed out:

> We will often get a new county executive or mayor on the supervisory board. Moreover, over time, we teach them about the bank and how it works. After a while, they come to see that it's more important to have a strong bank in the community than throw 1 or 2 million down a deficit hole that will be far less useful.

Two other bank managers suggested serving on the board instills certain values into its members.

> Sure some supervisory boards decide to pay out dividends, but most don't. And this has to do with the political culture on the board. Some boards are trained that there is no money available from the Sparkasse. In the cities with high deficits, board members know that a Sparkassen paying out 2, 3, or 5 million is not going to make much of a difference ... and so the parliamentary representatives on the supervisory boards say 'we are not going to pay out dividends'. While serving on the board they learn to believe it's better to keep the money in the Sparkasse system in order to strengthen the bank rather than give it to the cities.

Another CEO of one of the most profitable savings banks in Germany put it this way:

> I've seen a lot of county executives and mayors because I've been in the job for a long time. And the ones [politicians] who are sitting in the supervisory board would agree that we all share a foundational understanding that a Sparkasse is a bank and it is not set up to plug some random holes in a city or county budget.

The explanation given by respondents illustrates the banks' influence and highlights Lukes' second and third faces of power. In the second face, issues like dividends are not considered or debated because it is mostly kept off the agenda. Not only do bank managers not raise the topic, but neither the regional or national associations disclose systematic information about its members' dividend payments, thus making it difficult to assess how dividends affect banks or government owners. The third face of power is reflected in the socialization of board members to the Sparkassen's view that bank revenues are better spent on charity and increasing the institution's capital rather than on dividends to cities and counties.

There is also a more direct form of Sparkassen influence that's consistent with the first face of power. Even though local governments serve as the trustees of Sparkassen, governments and public officials depend on Sparkassen for their engagement in the community and the capital, which contributes to the economic health of the region. Politicians also depend on Sparkassen's support of local clubs and charities. Furthermore, politicians rely on bank management and the CEO in particular for information about the fiscal health of the institution. While supervisory board members are required by new EU rules to be knowledgeable about bank accounting and economics, mostrely on bank management for information and data. As one respondent put it, "It's rare for a supervisory board to challenge management's numbers. If the CEO says dividends will weaken the institution, board members are inclined to accept it."

In short, Sparkassen are effective in exerting power at the local level to maintain rules and norms that support and defend their business model. Local governments could demand their savings banks pay dividends. But with some notable exceptions politicians, regardless of their political party, do not press the issue and often refrain from challenging bank management's views on dividends. Respondents suggest that board members are deferential to bank management because of the bank's importance to the economic health of the region (the first face of power). Others suggested that the topic of dividends is kept off the agenda or board members do not bring it up (the second face of power). Moreover, CEOs and others suggest that once on the supervisory boards, parliamentarians become convinced of the banks' position on dividends (the third dimension of power). As a financial institution based in a town or city, it is not entirely surprising that Sparkassen have influence locally, but what explains their impact at the national and supranational level?

The next section turns to how small independent public banks are viewed as the most powerful lobbying group in Germany.

Power at the national level

The view of Sparkassen as among the most politically powerful entities in the world (Stevens & Steinauser 2013) is wildly overstated. In the case of EU efforts to create a European-wide banking union, the view among staff who work for MEPs that Sparkassen play an "outsized role." It is "outsized" because the opposition to public banks among European institutions and among lobby groups is so large: how could an entity like the DSGV manage to preserve Germany's public savings banks when the odds and the resources are so stacked against them? Savings banks mostly play defence, trying to prevent laws and regulations from being passed which undermine the banks. "Anytime we're successful, our critics claim we have too much influence", said one respondent. At the same time, the DSGV along with their credit union allies have managed to limit policies like European-wide deposit insurance that undermine their competitive advantage. So what does Sparkassen's power or influence look like?

Much of the research on Sparkassen's power and influence applies a principal–agent framework to how banks' governing structures contribute to political favouritism. Markgraf and Rosas (2019) argue that local politicians influence and benefit electorally from the lending behaviour of banks. A study published by the EZB argues that Sparkassen's lending behaviour is influenced by state elections (Schreiber 2018). And research by Deo *et al.* (2015) and Behn and Haselmann (2016) argue that decisions to resolve, merge, or recapitalize savings banks are influenced by the electoral concerns of political leaders. Such research on Sparkassen power infers abuses of authority and inefficiency caused by the close relationship between banks and their political owners. There have been financial scandals among some Sparkassen. However, incidents of abuse are isolated and not entirely surprising, given the number of Sparkassen and their independence. And while these studies of Sparkassen power are important, they share a very narrow view of power, one limited to Lukes' first face of power.

Moreover, such principal–agent accounts fail to explain the resiliency of public savings banks. Public savings banks in Germany are relatively stable and prosperous, while in other countries, similar banks with similar governing structures have disappeared or been transformed. Power matters. However, what accounts for Sparkassen's resiliency is institutional power: the influence that derives not from a single bank but from the network within which Sparkassen are embedded. Moreover, the power exercised through the larger network also reflects more than just a single face of Lukes' power typology.

The primary sources of Sparkassen's power stem from the banks' location within a broader institutional architecture. The first source of power and influence is geography. In 2018 there were 385 independent savings banks with 13,316 branches located in nearly every town and city in Germany. The S-Group paid €3.2 billion in income and revenue taxes in 2018. Also, the 301,600 S-Group employees work, vote, and pay taxes in each of these counties, cities and towns. Customers are primarily individuals and small- and medium-sized firms. More than three-quarters of German voters – 50 million – have savings accounts in savings banks or co-ops (Hesse *et al.* 2011). Combined, they make up about a third of all banking assets in Germany, more than the largest private banks (Howarth & Quaglia 2014; Hardie & Howarth 2013; Stevens & Steinhauser 2013). As one DSGV representative put it: "We have, I believe, a political influence because we are the central source of finance for small and medium-sized firms. And that means the government listens when we argue that a regulation threatens the stability of Sparkassen and by extension, the SME financing."

In explaining Sparkassen's power at the national level, representatives of private commercial and cooperative banks emphasize the geographic advantage and close relationship to local leaders. A representative from the Association of German Banks explained Sparkassen were powerful at the national level because of their local roots:

> It's local, it's regional, it's a politician you may know in the surroundings who is on the supervisory board, so it's just a matter of confidence. A private institution, well, it's offering online banking and things, there is just a certain perception of mistrust, I guess, which Sparkassen just don't have because it's all about: 'These are my friends, they are offering decent interest rates, I don't feel cheated by them and their institutional protection so they cannot fail by definition.'

The savings banks' connection to politicians increases banks' power and leverage, but it is more subtle and more systematic than the way it is typically discussed.

Having local political leaders on the boards of Sparkassen increases the public's trust and confidence in the savings banks. It establishes, in the minds of citizens, a close connection between the bank and the local governments. As has been pointed out, many view the church, city hall, and the Sparkasse as three co-equal institutions in a town or city. That connection fortifies and replicates a sense of loyalty and allegiance to Sparkassen, which private banks and cooperatives envy and often resent. In an expression of Lukes' second face of power, a private banker said, "We would love to end the regional principle or allow Sparkassen to be privatized, but we cannot even raise these issues for fear that it will anger the public".

The connection is promoted even further through the sponsoring but also through initiatives like *Weltspartag* or World Savings Day, an annual celebration since 1924 in which the importance of saving and, indirectly, the importance of Sparkassen is promoted in schools and communities. These efforts socialize the public – an example of the third face of power – at a very young age to the importance of saving and Sparkassen. The effort paid off. Sparkassen are among the most trusted institutions in Germany. The trust and loyalty ensure that even if a better interest rate or a cheaper account is available with a private competitor, customers are unlikely to leave the Sparkasse, which gives them an economic advantage. But there is a political benefit as well. Widespread trust among citizens and local political leaders from below translates into significant national and supranational power.

A respondent from the DSGV said Sparkassen's power derives from two factors: first, his members are deeply rooted in all of the regions in the country; and second, local authorities are represented on the supervisory board. He said,

> Those two factors combined make it possible for us to shape opinions really throughout Germany. Especially, in Germany, which is a federal state, where you have different power centres. If you want to be successful in any industry association you have to make sure you are in many power centres. In Munich, Dusseldorf, Berlin. And here we have that possibility via the representation in the regional associations and the many savings banks.

Geographic reach and local government representation also ensure that a large number of politicians from every region of the country and from every political party are socialized to the processes and perspectives of the country's public savings banks. As a supervisory board member pointed out, "It is rare to attend a political party conference where there are not members who serve or have served on a Sparkassen supervisory board. Every county executive and every mayor from a large city has served on his [sic] savings banks' supervisory board. These are the people who choose the national leaders and shape the party's platform."

In short, essential sources of Sparkassen's national power derives from the geographic representation and the public's and local politicians' trust and confidence in Sparkassen. Savings banks are significant players in every political jurisdiction in Germany. No other organization is located in as many communities in Germany or has as direct a connection with as many voters as savings banks. That connection enables Sparkassen to garner support from voters and politicians across the political spectrum whenever a national or EU issue arises that Sparkassen believe threatens their interests.

The S-Group network also provides Sparkassen with a vital source of influence. Individually, Sparkassen are decentralized, highly local and independent. Yet, Sparkassen are closely linked to each other through the 11 regional associations and one federal association. The associations monitor risk, hold regular meetings with their members, conduct audits, share information, provide training, and offer regulatory compliance assistance. The network's horizontal connections facilitated by their associations enables a single savings bank to tap the political resources of an entire region of savings banks. At the same time, Sparkassen are embedded within a vertical financial services network that also enables savings banks to amplify, coordinate and target their political voices in Berlin and Brussels. In short, Germany's public savings banks are nationally powerful not because of information asymmetries between politicians and the agency but because of where the banks fit within broader institutional architecture. The question considered in the next section is: how do they use this power?

Battle over banking union

One area where one can see how Sparkassen deploy their power and influence at the national and supranational level is during the policy processes to create a European banking union (EBU). The European Commission believes a banking union consisting of a single supervisory mechanism (SSM), a single resolution mechanism (SRM), and a European deposit insurance system (EDIS) are essential for European Monetary Union (EMU) to succeed. Scholars point to the global recession of 2007/08 and, later, the sovereign debt crisis, as justifications for the creation of a EBU (Gros & Schoenmaker 2013; Ioannidou 2012; Howarth & Quaglia 2014; Epstein & Rhodes 2016; Donnelly 2014). EBU is designed to interrupt the primary cause of the widespread contagion of global financial failure: the so-called "doom loop" or "vicious circle" in which banks and sovereigns depend on one another (Pisani-Ferry 2012).

Supervision was the first of the three "pillars" of formal EBU regulations to come into force. The goal of the SSM is to establish supervisory authority over all banks and ensure that "banks in the euro area stick to sound financial practices" (European Commission 2012). Michel Barnier, European Commission for Internal Market and Services, stated the "aim [of SSM] is to stop using taxpayers' money to bail out banks", therefore justifying the need for an integrated supervision system which places the European Central Bank as the central supervisor (European Commission 2012). The European Central Bank as this central supervisor, directly oversees Europe's largest or most significant banks, while also ultimately having authority over all banks in the euro area.

Although an essential first step, SSM alone was not enough – supervision is only effective when the supervisor has the authority to initiate a resolution in the case of a bank failure. The Single resolution mechanism complements the SSM, creating supranational institutions whose role it is to monitor systemic risks, conduct financial supervision, and oversee crisis management (European Commission 2016). The SRM, came into force 8 November 2013, and would be funded through proportional national contributions to a common fund.

Centralizing deposit insurance – the third leg of the banking union – was the next step the European Commission sought to take. Previous efforts to pass an EDIS in 2009 and 2014 had generated two EU Directives[18] that fell short of creating a single deposit insurance scheme. The Directives increased the harmonization of national deposit guarantee scheme rules and institutions, but member states were left in charge of their deposit insurance schemes. The Commission tried again in 2015 to generate similar outcomes, but it too failed. In 2016 Germany's chancellor, finance minister, and nearly all political parties in Germany's lower house, and the Bundestag uniformly condemned the EU's proposal (Plenarprotokoll 18/158 2016). Martin Zöllmer, a member of the Social Democratic Party (SPD), compared the proposal to placing a vampire in charge of a blood bank. In support of EDIS stood southern EU member states, the ECB, the IMF, EU Council President, and EU Commission, and members of the European Parliament. There are many reasons why EDIS failed but one is the skill with which Sparkassen and Germany's cooperatives were able to leverage their influence to resist EDIS, in order to protect their institutional protection scheme.

EU deposit insurance threatens the core of Sparkassen's (and cooperatives') institutional architecture. Deposit insurance insures depositors by requiring banks to set aside a certain amount of money into a fund that is then used to cover deposit holders in case of bank failure. However, Sparkassen employ an institutional protection scheme (IPS), which insures the institution, not depositors. The IPS means that public savings banks never fail. Instead, if an institution struggles, it is typically merged with another institution, and the other public savings banks in the region share the losses. Public savings banks also view IPS as a significant comparative advantage, allowing them to maintain high bond ratings, continuity for their customers, and unlimited depositor insurance.

For Sparkassen, EDIS threatens what the DSGV views as an essential part of their institutional identity. It is not surprising that when the Commission proposed EDIS in 2015, Sparkassen, along with cooperative banks, campaigned to block it. Given their size and limited resources (compared to private banks) the DSGV and cooperatives faced enormous odds.

Sparkassen staved off EDIS by leveraging their strong trust and popularity among the German population, their deep roots in every German community, and their organizational network. Statements from staff members who work for MEPs stressed that Sparkassen effectively used their vertical and horizontal networks to battle private banks and proponents of EDIS. Even as public savings banks were outspent on lobbying by private credit institutions, Sparkassen used their close connection to local and state governments to make their case before the European Commission and Parliament. It was thus not just the DSGV that pressed the case against EDIS, but representatives from Germany's 16 state governments who argued for the importance of IPS.

The DSGV was also effective at mobilizing their customers and communities. The DSGV sought to raise the saliency of deposit insurance among the public and policymakers which was no small task. Most people have little understanding or interest in the technical elements of the IPS or deposit insurance. When issues are highly salient it "expands the scope of conflict" (Schattschneider 1975). Politicians and interest groups take their message to the public through media and advertising campaigns. Alternatively, issues with low salience are what William Gormley (1986) calls "Board Room Politics" or what Pepper D. Culpepper (2011) terms "Quiet Politics". Low salience is the condition in which a lack of public awareness or interest enables policies to be more easily crafted by bureaucrats behind closed doors.

The DSGV along with its cooperative partners overcame their sizeable resource disadvantage by leveraging features that set Sparkassen apart from private banks to successfully raise the salience of EDIS (Cassell & Hutcheson 2019). Sparkassen and cooperatives convinced the German population to care about the arcane technical issues of deposit insurance. And as a result, policymakers were compelled to speak publicly on the issue and the European Commission was prevented from passing EDIS surreptitiously.

In the aftermath of the battle over EDIS private banking lobbyists and some European leaders expressed concern over the influence of Germany's public savings banks, suggesting Sparkassen had too much power. The battle over EDIS shows, however, that such accounts are overstated and simplistic. Globally, financial markets are dominated by a small number of private banking behemoths. Commercial banks in Europe outspend the DSGV on lobbying by nearly 30 to 1. The real story is that it is despite their enormous resource disadvantages, that Sparkassen were able to defend themselves by using different dimensions of power to influence the European Parliament and shape the public's understanding of EDIS. This is not to imply that Sparkassen are always successful. Adoption of SSM, SRM, and the elimination of explicit state guarantees of public banks are examples where Sparkasse were unsuccessful. Moreover, EDIS is unlikely to go away. And the European Union's fiscal efforts to prevent continent-wide economic depression in the wake of the Coronavirus pandemic may create the opening for a new European deposit insurance. However, EDIS underscores the fact that an important reason why Sparkassen continue to thrive is that despite being relatively small independent credit institutions, they can defend themselves even against formidable interests at the European-level. This is the power few credit institutions have access to in other countries.

Conclusion

Germany's public savings banks are resilient for a variety of reasons. Their unique business model complements national economic goals: adding economic value to local communities by bolstering national champions and SMEs, which have proven to be the engine of Germany's economy, and ensuring that economic prosperity is more widely distributed than in other countries. Moreover, Sparkassen's administrative features also serve as a buffer to global and domestic forces pushing toward an Anglo-Saxon model of finance. Their administrative structure creates proactive and efficient oversight and enables Sparkassen to enjoy the benefits of being small and local and large and national. However, neither Sparkassen's economic nor administrative characteristics would enable them to survive without also marshaling the political power to defend themselves against policies and laws that have undermined similar banks in other countries.

Scholars and journalists have written about Sparkassen's power and influence. However, much of the work takes a relatively narrow view of power, often focusing on the close connection between politicians and bank management. While this type of influence is important, this chapter illustrates how Sparkassen's political power is more pervasive, more complex, and more subtle than previously examined. Sparkassen exercise power and influence differently at different levels of government. At the local level, their influence is a function of their governance structure, their centrality in the economic life of the community, the close connection across a variety of demographic groups, and their branding. At the national level, Sparkassen's influence derives foremost from the size of the economic contribution to the country's economy. The number of assets, employees, and taxes paid makes the Sparkassen network a formidable interest group. But their power also stems from their close relationship to 50 million account holders/voters located in every political jurisdiction in the country, and the thousands of politicians whose first exposure to banking was as customers and then as members of the supervisory board of their local Sparkasse.

In short, an essential factor that enables Sparkassen to continue and even grow, despite global and domestic forces, is their ability to deploy different types or "faces" of power at different levels of government. We can see this in debates over the payout over dividends at the local level and European banking union at the national and supranational levels. The question going forward is whether Germany's public savings banks will be able to replenish the sources of their power; will they be able to adapt to a changing societal, economic and political landscape?

7
CONCLUSION

Interest in public banks is ascendant. The global recession in 2007/8 and the economic crises triggered by the coronavirus pandemic underscore the vulnerabilities of our financial systems and the role public banks play in bolstering and stabilizing economies. The policy scholar, John Kingdon (2011), argues in his seminal book *Agendas, Alternatives, and Public Policies* that major policy shifts occur when a problem stream, policy stream and political stream merge. Moreover, the merger does not occur by chance or naturally but is the result of three factors: (1) consistent and sustained action by advocates; (2) a triggering event; and (3) policy entrepreneurs capable of using the crisis to bring the streams together. Throughout Europe and Latin America public banks are playing a central role in governments' response to the economic impact of Covid-19 (IMF 2020; European Association of Public Banks 2020). Public banking advocates are pressing the case globally for the importance of public banking and political opportunities are opening up that had once been improbable. Drawing on Kingdon's insights, public banking's role in national economies is likely to grow particularly in countries that have traditionally resisted the idea like the United States. An understanding of public savings banks – how they operate and thrive – is now more important than ever.

A simple puzzle prompted this book. Sparkassen were established over two centuries ago to provide the poor and working-class with access to credit. Public savings banks populated nearly every European country, guaranteeing governments, firms, and citizens a stable source of credit and a safe place to deposit their savings. Yet, public savings banks have gone the way of the Dodo, morphing into enterprises that resemble commercial banks or disappearing entirely. The Great Recession of 2007/08 accelerated the process. Large multinational banks used their enormous public bailouts to expand market share, increase their size, and drive community banks and public savings banks out of the market. In Germany, this seemingly inexorable march toward greater consolidation of the banking sector appears to have been halted or slowed.

During a period of record-low interest rates and rising regulatory burdens, Germany's small, independent, local public savings banks remain a robust part of Germany's financial landscape. They are the primary bank for half of all German consumers, have 94 million accounts, are the main bank for 40 per cent of all German businesses, and account for 70 per cent of all lending to small and medium-sized enterprises (SMEs). They are the backbone of Germany's economy. They accomplished this while earning the highest credit rating scores, including an A+ rating from Fitch in December 2019. So, the puzzle is a relatively simple one: what accounts for the resilience of these small independent public credit institutions? What explains their ability to stay the course even as similar institutions in other countries disappear and "too big to fail" institutions appear ascendant?

The importance of the question extends well beyond the borders of Germany or Europe. Interest in public banks, particularly in the United States, has never been higher. Even before the coronavirus struck, the *American Banker* noted that public banking was gathering momentum across the country in response to a desire to keep funds within the state, cut ties with Wells Fargo, offer banking services to marijuana firms, and get better returns on public deposits (Alix 2018). California with its 37 million people has passed legislation that opens the door for public banks. The largest California cities are on their way to establishing public banks. Following on the heels of a number of state initiatives, New Jersey's governor formed a state-wide board in November 2019 to establish a public bank. The coronavirus that is crippling national economies is focusing attention on the weaknesses of the US financial system and the pitfalls of relying on private banks to provide public goods.

As part of the initial March 2020 $2 trillion response, the US passed the Paycheck Protection Program (PPP). The program allows small businesses to apply for federally-guaranteed loans of as much as $10 million with payments deferred for six months. Private banks responded to the proposal by immediately demanding the federal government double the rate of interest they can charge, from 0.5 per cent to 1 per cent to make it worth their while (Niquette & Sasso 2020). In addition, banks receive significant processing fees on these loans: 5 per cent on loans up to $350,000, 3 per cent on loans larger than that up to $2 million, and 1 per cent on loans between $2 million and $10 million. As one news account put it, "It's like an hour's work for a junior banker to process these loans and the bank can get between $10,000 and $100,000. And the fully guaranteed loans can be sold directly into the secondary market, so banks don't have to wait to recoup. It's about as free as money gets" (Dayen 2020). Yet in April 2020, commercial banks like Chase were failing to provide adequate lending to small businesses in time to save them (Cowley & Flitter 2020). The coronavirus will likely trigger policymakers in states and regions to exercise greater control and influence over the flow of credit and capital.

In this final chapter, I want to end with some reflections of broader relevance, particularly to efforts in the United States to establish public banks. The first section discusses the status of public banking in the United States, including recent legislative efforts to develop local and state public banks throughout the country through 2019; the second reviews the main arguments that I have set out; and the book closes with ten takeaways from my research that can inform debates over public banking in the United States and elsewhere.

Public banking in the United States

The public's trust in financial institutions plummeted in the wake of the Great Recession. A study published by the National Bureau of Economic Research found that confidence in financial institutions fell by 44 per cent in 2009 and 2010 (Stevenson & Wolfers 2011). The recession and public bailouts birthed the Occupy Wall Street movement and the Tea Party movement and laid the foundation for the rise in populism and the presidency of Donald Trump (Kumkar 2018; Judis 2016). The lesson many took from the Great Recession is that a public alternative to private commercial banks is essential, particularly in times of crisis (Marshall & Rochon 2019; Judd & McGhee 2011).

The United States has long had one public bank, the Bank of North Dakota (BND), a state bank founded in 1919 to protect local farmers and businesses from exploitation at the hands of commercial banks and grain operators (Junker 1989). The Nonpartisan League, a farmers' organization, created the bank to provide rural credit at cost, something commercial banks refused (Junker 1989: 4). The BND serves as the depository for all taxes and fees collected by the state and its public subdivisions as well as working funds for state institutions (except pension funds and other state-managed trusts). The bank uses those resources to fund development, agriculture, and small businesses in the state, mainly by working through the state's community banks (Schneiberg 2013: 281; Judd & McGhee 2011; Lessambo 2020).

Over its more than 100-year history, the BND successfully serviced community banks, enhanced competition among banks, lent to farmers and state businesses, provided consumer credit to students and homeowners, and helped local governments obtain capital at rates well below what commercial banks offer (Hussam 2018). Moreover, the BND's lending during the height of the financial crisis from 2007 to 2009 increased 35 per cent and experienced loan losses far lower than the average for similar-size banks (Judd & McGhee 2011; Macek 2019). The BND has served as a model for advocates of public banking in the United States (Schneiberg 2013; Macek 2019).

Since 2010, advocates have pushed for policies to establish local or state public banks in the United States (Judd & McGhee 2011; Centre for State Innovation 2010; Kodryzcki & Elmated 2011). The National Conference of State Legislatures tracks the number of state bills related to public banking (excluding infrastructure banks). Figure 7.1 illustrates the total number of bills per year introduced in state legislatures for the period 2010–17 and Figure 7.2 shows which regions of the country have seen efforts to establish a public bank.

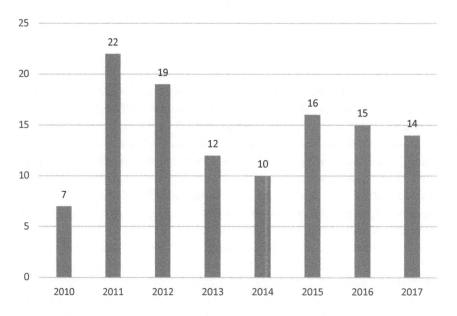

Figure 7.1 Annual public banking bills in the US state legislatures, 2010–17
Source: cited in Macek (2019: 38).

Bills introduced in state legislatures rose in 2011 and remained in the double digits throughout 2017. About half the laws call for the establishment of a public bank while the other half call for task forces or commissions to study their feasibility. Although interest has been high, success has been limited. Public banking advocates struggle to replicate the BND despite strong evidence of its success. Part of the challenge advocates face is the nature of the policy issue.

Public banking is an example of what James Q. Wilson refers to as "entrepreneurial politics", where a policy's costs are concentrated on a particular industry, profession, or locality. At the same time, benefits are dispersed across a large population (Wilson 2000: 77). Sparkassen benefit not only individual and business customers but also the region. The public benefits from the savings banks. Similarly, the research on the BND also points to the shared benefits that derive from a state-owned public bank (Judd & McGhee 2011; Kodryzcki & Elmated

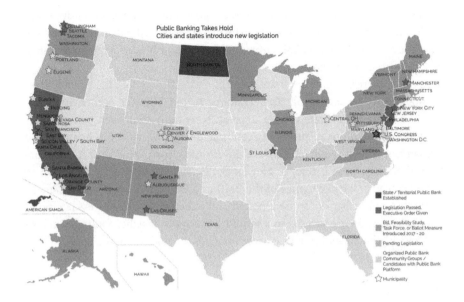

Figure 7.2 US cities and states that have introduced public banking legislation, 2020
Source: Public Banking Institute (2020).

2011). The perceived costs, on the other hand, are concentrated on a single industry with enormous influence on the political process. Private financial institutions and banks see public banking as a threat and lobby heavily against even proposals to study the issue. Indeed, in cases where legislators entertain the possibility of a public bank, there is always the stipulation that the public bank may never be allowed to compete with a private bank. The financial sector spent $2 billion on political activity from the beginning of 2015 to the end of 2016, including $1.2 billion in campaign contributions – more than twice the amount given by any other business sector (Schroeder 2017). Thus, despite the growing interest in alternatives to commercial banks, the political hurdles to establish a public bank are immense.

Nevertheless, in October 2019, California passed AB 857, the Public Banking Act, allowing the state to charter a public bank (Peltz 2019). The law creates a framework for cities and counties to apply for a public bank licence, which would require an independent board, a business plan, state Department of Business Oversight approval, and FDIC deposit insurance. The California law prohibits a public bank from competing with a private bank. Advocates in several California cities are now working to charter a municipal public bank, including in San Diego (Garrick 2020), Los Angeles (Reyes 2019), San Francisco (Wenus 2020), and

Oakland (Tadayon 2017). In New Jersey, the governor signed an executive order in November 2019 to create a board to form a state-owned public bank. And the legislature in the state of Washington authorized and funded a business plan, a necessary step toward applying for a state public bank charter.

In short, there is significant low-level exploration throughout the United States in establishing a public bank. The economic fallout from the coronavirus pandemic is likely to generate further interest. Now more than ever, policymakers require new solutions to promote economic development, retain financial and human assets, and reduce the cost of government borrowing for infrastructure (Detter & Fölser 2017; Katz & Nowak 2017). While not the only solution to these problems, the experience of the BND and Germany's Sparkassen, demonstrate that public banks can be a potent and effective way to address such policy challenges. Before turning to a set of takeaways or insights about Germany's Sparkassen, the next section briefly summarizes the findings of the book.

Key points

There are many ways to address the question of Sparkassen's remarkable resilience. Drawing on the work of public administration scholars including Steven Kelman (2005), Anne Khademian (2002), and James Q. Wilson (1989), I have argued that to understand how organizations work, we need the perspective of the operators, managers, executives within the organizations, and institutional actors that affect the organization's performance. Thus, to explain the performance of Germany's Sparkassen I interviewed Sparkassen and S-Group employees, managers, and executives, as well as institutional actors including customers, policymakers, journalists, scholars, and competitors. The answer that has emerged from those semi-structured conversations is three-fold.

First, Sparkassens' ability to survive and maintain themselves is a function of the economic value-added they provide to their local economic network consisting of firms, governments, civic associations, and Chambers of Commerce. Sparkassen have managed to turn a "boring business model" of taking deposits and making loans into a comparative advantage rather than a liability. Sparkassen need their regions, but what stands out is that the regions need the Sparkassen as well. Moreover, because of their central presence in the local network and their Hausbank relationship to SMEs, Sparkassen are the source of long-term (patient) capital to SMEs and the primary source of market and managerial information in the network. Yet, economic value alone is only part of the puzzle.

Administrative factors constitute a second component that undergirds Sparkassen success. The 385 savings banks form the foundation of one of the largest financial networks in the world. The network's structure complements

Germany's federalist system of local, state, and federal government. Each independent Sparkasse benefits from economies of scale – in areas of technology, marketing, regulatory compliance and loan approval – associated with a \$2.2 trillion financial holding company. The network also establishes and ensures a robust internal system of oversight built around an institutional protection scheme (IPS) rather than a deposit insurance scheme. The S-Group's IPS institutionalizes shared liability among each member of the network and establishes strong incentives for each bank to think about the health of the network as well as its own bank. As a result, the network includes a vigorous formal set of internal processes that ensure the integrity of the banks and the S-Group. Informal factors also provide for shared norms of accountability reinforced through extensive socialization within the network. The formal and informal internal systems of oversight are in addition to a comprehensive external oversight system consisting of local, state, federal, and European rules and regulations.

Finally, politics plays a role in Sparkassen's ability to survive and thrive in the increasingly global world of finance dominated by the largest players. In her remarkable book, *Politics and Banking: Ideas, Public Policy, and the Creation of Financial Institutions*, Susan Hoffmann (2001) underscores the importance that politics plays in the establishment of different types of depository institutions. Banks are not just economic entities. They are the product of political contestation. According to Hoffmann, credit unions, commercial banks, and savings and loans emerged from contentious political processes to solve specific public problems. In keeping with Hoffmann's insights, we can see Sparkassen also as the product of politics designed to address a set of public purposes. At the same time Sparkassen are themselves powerful actors that shape the policy process in essential and practical ways that enable them to defend and promote themselves.

Journalistic and scholarly accounts of Sparkassen's political influence are often too narrow and overly focused on the close local connections between political leaders and Sparkassen managers. I have argued that Sparkassen's success lies in their ability to exercise power and influence differently at different levels of government. At the local level, their influence is a function of their governance structure, their centrality in the economic life of the community, the close connection across a variety of demographic groups, and their branding. At the national level, Sparkassen's influence derives foremost from the size of their economic contribution to the country's economy. The number of assets, employees, and taxes paid makes the Sparkassen network a formidable interest group. But their power also stems from their close relationship to voters and politicians whose first exposure to banking is often as a Sparkassen customer. The question these findings raise is what insights they might offer to policymakers, advocates, and those interested in establishing a public bank elsewhere.

Ten policy takeaways

1. *Not all public banks are the same.* Critics of public banks often speak about them as if they are monolithic. Sparkassen are an example of a local retail-oriented public bank in which local governments serve as trustees, though not owners of the institution. Sparkassen are not the equivalent of a government asset that can be bought or sold like a building or plot of land. Instead, Sparkassen are more akin to a utility or fire department that might be merged with another jurisdiction but never sold. The BND is a state-level wholesale oriented lender governed by leaders appointed at the state level. Germany also has development banks with far closer ties to the government, and state-level public banks that operate and are governed differently from public savings banks. In short, one can establish a public bank with a mission, governance structure, and jurisdiction designed for a specific constituency.

2. *Profits and public goals are compatible.* Sparkassen are for-profit institutions but not profit-maximizing institutions. Sparkassen and the BND demonstrate that it is possible to pursue a set of public purposes while operating as a for-profit institution. The Sparkassen's public mission enhances the banks' bottom line in several ways. The public mission gives banks the flexibility to extend credit on terms that allow firms and individuals to adopt a long-term time horizon. The public purpose enables savings banks to play a specific proactive role in promoting the region's economic well-being. Finally, the public mission strengthens the bond between the bank and the local economic network. Each of these elements of the public mission help savings banks' long-term performance.

3. *Performance should be based on mission, not profits.* Comparing public with commercial banks based on profits or share value fails to take into account a public banks' mission. Public banks are not profit-maximizing institutions. Sparkassen's value-added includes ensuring firms stable access to long-term credit at competitive rates, generating and sharing market and managerial information within the local economic network, and supporting the civic and social life of the community. Assessing the performance of a public bank requires a broader lens than just profits.

4. *Public banks improve competition.* Banking competition has declined in many countries, including the United States. Small and community banks, in particular, have lost market share to large commercial banks from out of the state. Declines in competition correspond to decreases in lending to SMEs and increases in the cost of borrowing. Commercial banks – driven to maximize their profits – abandoned poorer parts of the country in the aftermath of German unification and in the wake of the financial crisis. Sparkassen's presence ensured that governments, firms, and households continued to

have access to credit at competitive rates. Data from Germany and North Dakota find that public banks increase competition and strengthen the health of local financial markets.

5. *Public banks are a useful indirect tool for economic development.* Economic development is often a function of direct public subsidies or tax abatements to firms. Sparkassen illustrate how governments can deploy public banks to support a regional economy indirectly: by increasing local liquidity through a steady flow of long-term credit to SMEs, making funds available to governments for a long-term infrastructure project, being at the centre of the local economic network, and keeping assets in the region. In the case of the BND and some Sparkassen, the banks also returned a nice dividend to the governments' general funds.

6. *Public banks are a source of financial inclusion.* Individuals and households who are poor, immigrants, or have been incarcerated suffer from a lack of credit or banking options. Sparkassen's experience demonstrates that public banks are an important source of financial inclusion.

7. *Public banks are efficient.* Sparkassen and the BND demonstrate that public banks can operate extremely efficiently. The administrative costs of Germany's public savings banks are below those of commercial banks. Efficiency is a function of a variety of factors. However, the most important are laws and policies that shield a bank's management from political influence. There is a clear and formal separation between Sparkassen's supervisory committee and their management committee. Laws and policies prohibit politicians from intervening in the management of Sparkassen.

8. *Effective oversight and accountability are a function of administration.* Sparkassen, like all German banks, are subject to state, federal, and European regulations. However, because of formal and informal administrative factors, public savings banks largely avoided the risky mistakes that brought down larger institutions in the lead up to the financial crisis.

9. *Administration can be a competitive advantage for public banks.* Administration enables the relatively small savings banks to retain their independence yet benefit from economies of scale that stem from being part of one of the largest financial networks in the world. As a result, banks can make decisions flexibly and quickly without having to seek approval from a central office. At the same time, expenses associated with branding and marketing, regulatory compliance, training, and IT are spread across the entire network.

10. *Politics matters.* Finally, public savings banks' success is not merely the result of market factors but power and politics. In 2016 the private financial industry spent $2 billion to influence US elections and shape the policy process. Like their private competitors, Sparkassen recognize the importance of developing and exercising influence at all levels of government. Public savings banks do

not allow themselves to be passive recipients of policy outcomes. They tap into different "faces" of power to promote and defend themselves.

During the process of completing this book, the world is in the middle of a global pandemic that is quickly morphing into an economic crisis on a par with the Great Depression of the 1930s. Germany's economy is predicted to shrink by between 7.2 per cent and 20.6 per cent (Hallam 2020). In response, Germany's federal government turned to its public banks to address the crisis. In the United States the government struggled to get credit into the hands of businesses because firms had to apply to private banks who quickly put up barriers. Germany took a different path. The German parliament gave authority to the Kreditanstalt für Wiederaufbau (KfW), the national public development bank, to lend a half a trillion euros, guaranteed by the federal government, to small and large firms (Carrel 2020). Since the KfW does not have branches, a customer applies for federal loans through their Hausbank which in most cases is a Sparkasse or cooperative. As the central players in their local economic network, Sparkassen are instrumental in helping firms navigate the process for getting assistance. Sparkassen also suspended principle and interest payments on all business loans for three months. And Sparkassen rolled out bridging loans to cover firms' expenses while they wait for federal support to arrive. As is noted throughout this book, what sets Sparkassen apart from their commercial counterparts is that the public banks are not profit-maximizing institutions. Instead they are for-profit institutions charged with protecting the interests of their customer and communities. As a result, Germany is predicted to be a "Post-coronavirus winner" because banks have not put up barriers to funding (Carletti *et al.* 2020). While companies in the United States and the UK have struggled to get state support, Germany's *Mittelstand* companies praise the government's "hands-on approach". It remains unclear how the economic crisis will play out. However, according to Ana Botin, chairman of Banco Santander SA, Spain's largest lender, Germany's loan programme should become the "benchmark" for the rest of Europe (Look & Nicola 2020).

Public banks are not the only banking institutions addressing economic crisis triggered by the Covid-19 pandemic. Credit institutions of all types have played a role in each countries' efforts to minimize the recession. This book is not an argument in favour of any one type of bank. Instead the book explains the resiliency of these small, independent, public credit institutions that have existed in Germany and German territories for more than 250 years. And what the Great Recession of 2007/08 and the pandemic recession of 2020 reveal is that while their business model may be "boring", Sparkassen are sources of stability under normal circumstances and financial first responders in times of crisis.

NOTES

1. For a review see Beck *et al.* (2009) and Simpson (2013).
2. Two particularly popular books are Michael Lewis, *The Big Short* (New York: Norton, 2010) and Andrew Ross Soskin, *Too Big to Fail* (New York: Viking, 2009). Successful movies include *Inside Job*, *The Big Short* and *Margin Call*. Two podcasts by Ira Glas, Adam Davidson and Alex Blumberg that do an excellent job of describing the financial crisis are: "Bad Bank" (NPR: *This American Life*, 27 February 2009) and "The Giant Pool of Money" (NPR: *This American Life*, 9 May 2009).
3. Alter *et al.* (1992) note the early American mutual savings banks were part of the same movement. Kohl (2017) and Gorsky (1998) point to similarities to the Friendly Societies in England in the nineteenth century.
4. Translated from "*Ohne ein Girokonto lässt sich das Leben kaum meistern. Wer keines besitzt, bekommt keinen Job, findet keine Wohnung, erhält keine Steuerrückzahlung*".
5. In Germany's Constitution or Basic Law, the regional principle is based on Article 28(2) which specifies the conditions and privileges of state and local self-governance. Courts have ruled that Sparkassen are included.
6. Five Sparkassen located in northern Germany including the city of Hamburg are private savings banks with governance structures that correspond to those of a private corporation. These "Independent Sparkassen" founded at the end of the eighteenth century by private individuals are still required to pursue a public mission despite their private identity (Schackmann-Fallis *et al.* 2017).
7. The exchange rate per child was up to 2,000 East German marks and persons older than 60 could exchange up to 6,000 marks. Higher amounts were exchanged 2:1.
8. For a list of the organizations supported by the Sparkassen Oberhessen, see https://neu. einfach-gut-machen.de/oberhessen/projekttraeger.
9. Bayern LB, HELABA, SaarLB, LBBW, Nord/LB and LB Berlin.
10. For a description of development banks in Germany see work by the Bundesverband Öffentlicher Banken Deutschlands ("Bundesverband Öffentlicher Banken Deutschlands, VÖB, e.V. - Fördergeschäft / Förderbanken," n.d.).
11. See https://eur-lex.europa.eu/legal-content/EN/ TXT/?uri=CELEX:02013R0575-20180101.
12. Europe's financial supervisory framework includes the European Banking Authority (EBA), the European Insurance and Occupational Pension Authority (EIOPA) and the European Securities and Markets Authority (ESMA).
13. The average size of public savings banks in Germany is $2.8 billion.
14. See https://www.s-hochschule.de/.

15. Cooperatives are embedded within a network of their own called Genossenschaftliche FinanzGruppe Volksbanken Raiffeisenbanken.
16. This contrasts to community banks in the United States which are exempt from many federal banking regulations. A Congressional report noted that "Of the 14 'major' rules issued by banking regulators under the Dodd-Frank Act (P.L. 111-203), 13 either include an exemption for small banks or are tailored to reduce the cost for small banks to comply" (Hoskins & Labonte 2015: 1).
17. Translated from "Soweit der verbliebene Betrag nicht zur weiteren Stärkung der Rücklagen benötigt wird, können aus ihm in angemessenem Umfang Abführungen an den Träger erfolgen".
18. Directive 2009/14/EC and Directive 2014/49/EU.

REFERENCES

Albert, M. 1993. *Capitalism vs. Capitalism: How America's Obsession with Individual Achievement and Short-Term Profit has led it to the Brink of Collapse*. New York: Four Walls Eight Windows.

Alessandri, P. & B. Nelson 2015. "Simple banking: profitability and the yield curve". *Journal of Money, Credit and Banking* 47(1): 143–75.

Alessandrini, P., G. Calcagnini & A. Zazzaro 2008. "Asset restructuring strategies in bank acquisitions: does distance between dealing partners matter?" *Journal of Banking & Finance* 32(5): 699–713. https://doi.org/10.1016/j.jbankfin.2007.05.008

Aliber, R. & C. Kindleberger 2015. *Manias, Panics and Crashes: A History of Financial Crises*, seventh edition. London: Palgrave Macmillan.

Allen, F., E. Carletti & A. Leonello 2011. "Deposit insurance and risk taking". *Oxford Review of Economic Policy* 27(3): 464–78. https://doi.org/10.1093/oxrep/grr022

Amy, D. 2011. *Government is Good: An Unapologetic Defense of a Vital Institution*. Indianapolis, IN: Dog Ear Pub.

Arnold, M. 2016. "Überlastete Banken; Sparkasse öffnet Filiale nur für Flüchtlinge". *Die Welt Online*, 16 February; https://www.welt.de/regionales/nrw/article152285586/Sparkasse-oeffnet-Filiale-nur-fuer-Fluechtlinge.html.

Atzler, E. 2016. "Hohe Gewinne, kaum Dividenden: Sparkassen geizen bei Ausschüttungen". *Handelsblatt Online*, 5 July; https://www.wiwo.de/hohe-gewinne-kaum-dividenden-Sparkassen-geizen-bei-ausschuettungen/13832586.html.

Audretsch, D., E. Lehmann & J. Schenkenhofer 2018. "Internationalization strategies of hidden champions: lessons from Germany". *Multinational Business Review* 26(1): 2–24.

Ayadi, R. *et al.* (eds) 2010. *Investigating Diversity in the Banking Sector in Europe: Key Developments, Performance and Role of Cooperative Banks*. Brussels: CEPS.

Bachrach, P. & M. Baratz 1962. "Two faces of power". *American Political Science Review* 56(4), 947–52. https://doi.org/10.2307/1952796

Baker, W. 1990. "Market networks and corporate behavior". *American Journal of Sociology* 96(3): 589–625.

Barth, J., S. Trimbath & G. Yago (eds) 2004. *The Savings and Loans Crisis: Lessons from a Regulatory Failure*. Santa Monica, CA: Kluwer Academic.

Behn, M. & R. Haselmann 2016. "The political economy of bank bailouts". *SAFE Working Paper* 133. Frankfurt: Centre for Financial Studies and Goethe University Frankfurt.

Behr, P. & R. Schmidt 2016. "The German banking system". In T. Beck & B. Casu (eds), *The Palgrave Handbook of European Banking*, 541–66. London: Palgrave Macmillan. https://doi.org/10.1057/978-1-137-52144-6_21

Berghoff, H. 2006. "The end of family business? The Mittelstand and German capitalism in transition, 1949–2000". *Business History Review* 80(2): 263–95. https://doi.org/10.1017/S000768050000012X.

Berlemann, M., M. Oestmann & M. Thum 2014. "Demographic change and bank profitability: empirical evidence from German savings banks". *Applied Economics* 46(1): 79–94. https://doi.org/10.1080/00036846.2013.829262.

Bertelsman Stiftung 2019. *Kommunaler Finanzreport 2019.*

Biswas, R. & H. Löchel 2001. "Recent trends in US and German banking: convergence or divergence?" *Arbeitsberichte der Hochschule für Bankwirtschaft* 29. Frankfurt am Main: Hochschule für Bankwirtschaft (HfB). http://hdl.handle.net/10419/27797

Black, W. 2013. *The Best Way to Rob a Bank is to Own One: How Corporate Executives and Politicians Looted the S&L Industry.* Austin, TX: University of Texas Press.

Blackbourn, D. 1977. "The Mittelstand in German society and politics, 1871–1914". *Social History* 2(4): 409–33.

Blyth, M. 2015. *Austerity: The History of a Dangerous Idea.* Oxford: Oxford University Press.

BMWi 2018. "SMEs are driving economic success". *BMWi Report.* Berlin: BMWi (Bundesministerium für Wirtschaft und Energie); https://www.bmwi.de/Redaktion/EN/Publikationen/Mittelstand/driving-economic-success-sme.pdf?__blob=publicationFile&v=2

Bofinger, P. *et al.* 2008. *Das deutsche Finanzsystem Effizienz steigern – Stabilität erhöhen Expertise im Auftrag der Bundesregierung.* Wiesbaden: Sachverständigenrat zur Begutachtung der gesamtwirtschaftlichen Entwicklung, Statistisches Bundesamt.

Borio, C., L. Gambacorta & B. Hofmann 2015. "The influence of monetary policy on bank profitability". *BIS Working Paper* 514. Basel: Bank of International Settlements. https://www.bis.org/publ/work514.pdf.

Bozeman, B. 2002. "Public–value failure: when efficient markets may not do". *Public Administration Review* 62(2): 145–61.

Brämer, P. *et al.* 2010. "Der öffentliche Auftrag der deutschen Sparkassen aus der Perspektive des Stakeholder-Managements". *Zeitschrift Für Öffentliche Und Gemeinwirtschaftliche Unternehmen* 33(4): 311–32.

Braun, B. 2018. "Central banking and the infrastructural power of finance: the case of ECB support for repo and securitization markets". *Socio-Economic Review*, 0(0), 1–24. https://doi.org/10.31235/osf.io/nrmt4

Braunberger, G. 2017, February 2. Niedrigzins: Deutsche Banken leiden besonders. *Frankfurter Allgemeine Zeitung*, 2 February. https://www.faz.net/1.4817477.

Bresler, N., I. Größl & A. Turner 2006. "The role of German savings banks in preventing financial exclusion". In L. Anderloni, E. Carluccio & M. Braga (eds), *New Frontiers in Banking Services*, 247–69. Frankfurt: Springer.

Brewster, B., J. Butler & A. Watkins 2019. "Eliminating biases that jeopardize audit quality". *Journal of Accountancy*, August 2019. https://www.journalofaccountancy.com/issues/2019/aug/biases-jeopardize-audit-quality.html.

Buell, T. 2016. "ECB president says crowded banking sector hurts profits". *Wall Street Journal*, 22 September.

Bülbül, D., R. Schmidt & U. Schüwer 2013. "Savings banks and cooperative banks in Europe". *White Paper Series* 5. Frankfurt: Sustainable Architecture for Finance in Europe (SAFE).

Butzbach, O. 2008. "European savings banks and the future of public banking in advanced economies: the cases of France, Germany, Italy and Spain". In K. von Mettenheim & M. Del Tedesco Lins (eds), *Government Banking: New Perspectives on Sustainable*

Development and Social Inclusion From Europe and South America, 85–126. Berlin: Konrad Adenauer Stiftung.

Brown, W. 2015. *Undoing the Demos: Neoliberalism's Stealth Revolution*. New York: Zone Books.

Calomiris, C. 1990. "Is deposit insurance necessary? A historical perspective". *Journal of Economic History* 50(2): 283–95.

Carles Maixé-Altés, J. 2010. "Competition and choice: banks and savings banks in Spain". *Journal of Management History* 16(1): 29–43.

Carletti, E., H. Hakenes & I. Schnabel 2005. "The privatization of Italian savings banks: a role model for Germany?" *Quarterly Journal of Economic Research* 74(4): 32–50.

Carletti, E. *et al.* 2020. "Germany will be a post-Coronavirus winner". Bloomberg. Com, 9 April. https://www.bloomberg.com/opinion/articles/2020-04-09/covid-19-germany-will-be-a-post-coronavirus-winner.

Cassell, M. 2002. *How Governments Privatize: The Politics of Divestment in the United States and Germany*. Washington, DC: Georgetown University Press.

Cassell, M. 2016. "A tale of two crises: Germany's *Landesbanken* and the United States' Savings and Loans". *Journal of Banking Regulation* 17(1/2): 73–89.

Cassell, M. & A. Hutcheson 2019. "Explaining Germany's position on European Banking Union". *German Politics* 28(4): 1–21.

Cassiman, B., M. Di Guardo & G. Valentini 2009. "Organising R&D projects to profit from innovation: insights from co-opetition". *Long Range Planning* 42(2): 216–33.

Centre for State Innovation 2010. *Washington State Bank Analysis*. http://leg.wa.gov/JointCommittees/Archive/IFTF/Documents/2011Aug22/CSI-Analysis.pdf

Choulet, C. 2016. "German Sparkassen: a model to follow?" *Conjuncture*. Paris: BNP Paribas. https://economic-research.bnpparibas.com/Views/DisplayPublication.aspx?type=document&IdPdf=28761.

Choulet, C. 2017. "Institutional protection systems: are they banking groups?" *Conjuncture*. Paris: BNP Paribas.

Christians, U. 2015. *Wachstums-, Erfolgs- und Risikoentwicklung von Banken in peripheren Regionen: Eine Kennzahlenanalyse am Beispiel der Kreditgenossenschaften und Sparkassen in Brandenburg in mittelfristiger Perspektive*. Berlin: Logos Verlag.

Coppola, F. 2015. "Breaking up Deutsche Bank". *Forbes*, 21 April; https://www.forbes.com/sites/francescoppola/2015/04/21/breaking-up-deutsche-bank/#11a53de34f3a.

Coppola, F. 2017. "The wondrous German public sector banks aren't all they are cracked up to be". *Forbes*, 24 October; https://www.forbes.com/sites/francescoppola/2017/10/24/the-wondrous-german-public-sector-banks-arent-all-they-are-cracked-up-to-be/.

Cowley, S. & E. Flitter 2020. "Frenzy and desperation as small businesses grab for government aid". *New York Times*, 3 April; https://www.nytimes.com/2020/04/03/business/sba-loans-coronavirus.html.

Crouch, C. & W. Streeck (eds) 1997. *Political Economy of Modern Capitalism: Mapping Convergence and Diversity*. London: Sage.

Culpepper, P. 2011. *Quiet Politics and Business Power: Corporate Control in Europe and Japan*. New York: Cambridge University Press.

D'Acunto, F., M. Prokopczuk & M. Weber 2013. "Antisemitism affects households' investments". *SSRN Electronic Journal*. 10.2139/ssrn.2368073.

Dahl, R. 2005. *Who Governs? Democracy and Power in an American City*, second edition. New Haven, CT: Yale University Press.

Das, S. 2010. *Traders, Guns & Money: Knowns and Unknowns in the Dazzling World of Derivatives*. Harlow: Financial Times Prentice Hall.

Dayen, D. 2020. "Unsanitized: why banks don't want to help small businesses". *The American Prospect*, 3 April; https://prospect.org/api/content/0d696628-75b7-11ea-8b92-1244d5f7c7c6/.

Deeg, R. 1999. *Finance Capitalism Unveiled: Banks and the German Political Economy*. Ann Arbor, MI: University of Michigan Press.

Deeg, R. 2007. "Complementarity and institutional change in capitalist systems". *Journal of European Public Policy* 14(4): 611–30.

Deeg, R. 2010. "Industry and finance in Germany since unification". *German Politics & Society* 28(2): 116–29.

Deeg, R. & I. Hardie 2016. "What is patient capital and who supplies it?" *Socio-Economic Review* 14(4): 627–45. https://doi.org/10.1093/ser/mww025.

Deeg, R. & S. Donnelly 2016. "Banking union and the future of alternative banks: revival, stagnation or decline?" *West European Politics* 39(3): 585–604.

Deo, S. *et al.* 2015. "Preventing German bank failures: federalism and decisions to save troubled banks". *Politische Vierteljahresschrift* 56: 159–81.

Der Tagesspiegel 2009. "Sparkassen trotz Krise mit Milliardengewinn". *Der Tagesspiegel*, 18 March; https://www.tagesspiegel.de/wirtschaft/finanzen/finanzkrise-Sparkassen-trotz-krise-mit-milliardengewinn/1476720.html.

Detter, D. & S. Fölster 2017. *The Public Wealth of Cities: How to Unlock Hidden Assets to Boost Growth and Prosperity*. Washington, DC: Brookings Institution Press.

Deutsche Bundesbank 2005. "Geldpolitik, bankgeschäft und kapitalmarkt". *Monthly Report*. Frankfurt: Deutsche Bundesbank.

Deutsche Bundesbank 2012. "Long-term developments in corporate financing in Germany: evidence based on the financial accounts". *Monthly Report*. Frankfurt: Deutsche Bundesbank.

Deutsche Bundesbank 2017. "Results of the 2017 low-interest-rate survey." Frankfurt: Deutsche Bundesbank; https://www.bundesbank.de/en/press/press-releases/results-of-the-2017-low-interest-rate-survey-667444.

Deutsche Bundesbank 2018. "The performance of German credit institutions in 2017". *Monthly Report*. Frankfurt: Deutsche Bundesbank; https://www.bundesbank.de/resource/blob/760004/6d8b3367ff98c77e715eac6c7c12bfc7/mL/2018-09-ertragslage-data.pdf.

DeYoung, R., D. Glennon & P. Nigro 2008. "Borrower–lender distance, credit scoring, and loan performance: evidence from informational-opaque small business borrowers". *Journal of Financial Intermediation* 17(1): 113–43.

Dietrich, D. & U. Vollmer 2012. "Are universal banks bad for financial stability? Germany during the world financial crisis". *Quarterly Review of Economics and Finance* 52(2): 123–34.

Dönch, U. *et al.* 2009. "Wie heil ist die Sparkassen-Welt?" *FOCUS Online*, 17 August; https://www.focus.de/finanzen/news/finanzkrise-wie-heil-ist-die-Sparkassen-welt_aid_426502.html.

Donahue, J. 1999. *The Privatization Decision: Public Ends, Private Means*. New York: Basic Books.

Donges, J., J. Eekhoff & W. Möschel (eds) (2001). *Privatisierung von Landesbanken und Sparkassen*. Frankfurter Inst. - Stiftung Marktwirtschaft und Politik.

Donnelly, S. 2014. "Banking union in Europe and implications for financial stability". *Studia Diplomatica* 67(2), 21–34.

DSGV 2018. *Sparkassenrangliste 2018*; https://www.dsgv.de/Sparkassen-finanzgruppe/organisation/Sparkassen.html.

Dustmann, C. *et al.* 2014. "From sick man of Europe to economic superstar: Germany's resurgent economy". *Journal of Economic Perspectives* 28(1): 167–88.

Dyer, J. & H. Singh 1998. "The relational view: cooperative strategy and sources of interorganizational competitive advantage". *Academy of Management Review* 23(4): 660.

Dyson, K. 1992. *The Politics of German Regulation*. Aldershot: Dartmouth.

Economist, The 2014. "German lessons". *The Economist*, 12 July; https://www.economist.com/business/2014/07/12/german-lessons.

Edelman, M. 1985. *The Symbolic Uses of Politics*. Urbana, IL: University of Illinois Press.

Edwards, J. & K. Fischer 1996. *Banks, Finance and Investment in Germany*. Cambridge: Cambridge University Press.

Eisingerich, A., S. Bell & P. Tracey 2010. "How can clusters sustain performance? The role of network strength, network openness, and environmental uncertainty". *Research Policy* 39(2): 239–53.

Elsas, R. & J. Krahnen 2004. "The universal banks and relationships with firms". In J. Krahnen & R. Schmidt (eds), *The German Financial System*. Oxford: Oxford University Press.

Engelhard, M. 2018. "Small credit institutions and proportionality: the perspective after the risk reduction package". CLES/EBI-Conference, Ljubljana, October 2018; https://ebi-europa.eu/wp-content/uploads/2018/07/Michael-Engelhard-Small-credit-institutions-and-proportionality.pdf.

Epstein, R. & M. Rhodes 2016. "The political dynamics behind Europe's new banking union". *West European Politics* 39(3), 415–37. https://doi.org/10.1080/01402382.2016.1143238.

European Central Bank 2016. "Guide on the approach for the recognition of institutional protection schemes (IPS) for prudential purposes". *Banking Supervision*. Brussels: Publications Office of the European Union.

European Commission 2009. Report of the High-Level Group on Financial Supervision in the EU chaired by Jacques de Larosière; http://ec.europa.eu/internal_market/finances/docs/de_larosiere_report_en.pdf.

European Commission 2012. Commission proposes new ECB powers for banking supervision as part of a banking union; http://eeas.europa.eu/archives/delegations/australia/documents/press_corner/i12_953_en.pdf.

European Commission 2013. "Europeans, the European Union and the crisis". *Standard Eurobarometer* 79. Brussels: Directorate General for Communication.

Ewing, J. 2019. "Deutsche Bank's turnaround costs lead to big loss". *New York Times*, 24 July; https://www.nytimes.com/2019/07/24/business/deutsche-bank-earnings-loss.html.

Feigenbaum, H. & J. Henig 1994. "The political underpinnings of privatization: a typology". *World Politics* 46(2): 185–208.

Finanzgruppe Deutscher Sparkassen- und Giroverband 2010. "Zur geschichte der Sparkassen in Deutschland." *Fakten, Analysen, Positionen* 45. Berlin: Deutscher Sparkassen- und Giroverband e.V.

Finanzgruppe Deutscher Sparkassen- und Giroverband 2018. *Inside the Savings Banks Finance Group*. Berlin: Deutscher Sparkassen- und Giroverband e.V.

Fleming, S. & J. Brunsden 2020. "EU banking agency criticised over director's move to lobby group". *Financial Times*, 11 May; https://www.ft.com/content/835bba98-8af3-444b-87fd-4b14ba822783.

Friedman, M. 1993. "Why government is the problem". *Essays in Public Policy* 39. Stanford, CA: Hoover Institution on War, Revolution, and Peace, Stanford University.

Fritsch, M. & M. Wyrwich 2020. "Does successful innovation require large urban areas? Germany as a counterexample". *Jena Economic Research Papers* 4. Jena: Friedrich Schiller University; http://www2.wiwi.unijena.de/Papers/jerp2020/wp_2020_004.pdf.

Führer, K. 2001. "Pawning in German working-class life before the First World War". *International Review of Social History* 46(1): 29–44.

Garicano, L. 2012. "Five lessons from the Spanish Cajas debacle for a new euro-wide supervisor". In T. Beck (ed.), *Banking Union For Europe: Risks and Challenges*, 79–86. London: Centre for Economic Policy Research.

Garrick, D. 2020. "San Diego could create public bank; 4 council members want to spend $250K on feasibility study". *San Diego Union-Tribune*, 3 February.

Gärtner, S. 2008. *Ausgewogene Strukturpolitik: Sparkassen aus regionalökonomischer Perspektive*. Berlin: LIT-Verl.

Gärtner, S. 2010. "Die räumliche dimension im bankgeschäft: regionale finanzintermediäre in strukturschwachen Räumen". In U. Christians & K. Hempel (eds), *Unternehmensfinanzierung und Region: Finanzierungsprobleme mittelständischer Unternehmen und Bankpolitik in peripheren Wirtschaftsräumen*, 205–30. Hamburg: Kovač.

Gärtner, S. 2017. *Raum und Banken: Zur Funktionsweise regionaler Banken*. Baden-Baden: Nomos.

Gärtner, S. & U. Christians 2015. *Wo sind die profitablen Sparkassen zu finden? Ertragskraft, Kreditrisiko und Eigenkapitalausstattung der Sparkassen in Abhängigkeit vom regionalen Standort*, Volume 11. Aachen: Shaker Verlag.

Gärtner, S. & F. Flögel 2017. *Raum und Banken: Zur Funktionsweise regionaler Banken*. Baden-Baden: Nomos.

Gaventa, J. 1982. *Power and Powerlessness: Quiescence and Rebellion in an Appalachian Valley*. Urbana, IL: University of Illinois Press.

Gerschenkron, A. 1989. *Bread and Democracy in Germany*. Ithaca, NY: Cornell University Press.

Gerschenkron, A. 1962. *Economic Backwardness in Historical Perspective: A Book of Essays*. Cambridge, MA: Harvard University Press.

Gjelten, T. 2008. "In Germany, a sound banking system amid turmoil". *National Public Radio*, 9 October; https://www.npr.org/templates/story/story.php?storyId=95567816.

Glaser, B. & A. Strauss 2009. *The Discovery of Grounded Theory: Strategies for Qualitative Research*. New Brunswick, NJ: Aldine.

Göbel, H. 2015. "Wirtschaftsforscher: lokalpolitiker nutzen Sparkassen zur wiederwahl". *Frankfurter Allgemeine Zeitung*, 26 November; http://www.faz.net/1.3932225.

Gook, B. 2018. "Backdating German neoliberalism: ordoliberalism, the German model and economic experiments in eastern Germany after 1989". *Journal of Sociology* 54(1), 33–48; https://doi.org/10.1177/1440783318759085.

Gormley, W. 1986. "Regulatory issue networks in a federal system". *Polity* 18(4): 595–620. https://doi.org/10.2307/3234884.

Gormley, W. (ed.) 1991. *Privatization and its Alternatives*. Madison, WI: University of Wisconsin Press.

Grahl, J. & P. Teague 2004. "The German model in danger". *Industrial Relations Journal* 35(6): 557–73.

Gros, D. & D. Schoenmaker 2014. "European deposit insurance and resolution in the banking union". *JCMS: Journal of Common Market Studies* 52(3): 529–46; https://papers.ssrn.com/abstract=2052886.

Gubitz, B. 2013. *Das Ende des Landesbankensektors: Der Einfluss von Politik, Management und Sparkassen*. Wiesbaden: Springer Gabler.

Gulick, L. & L. Urwick 1937. *Notes on the Theory of Organization*. New York: Columbia University, Institute of Public Administration; https://books.google.com/books?id=iTFKMwEACAAJ.

Guinnane, T. 2002. "Delegated monitors, large and small: Germany's banking system, 1800–1914". *Journal of Economic Literature* 40(1): 73–124.

Hackenthal, A. 2004. "German banks and banking structure". In J. Krahnen & R. Schmidt (eds), *The German Financial System*, 71–104. Oxford: Oxford University Press.

Hackethal, A., R. Schmidt & M. Tyrell 2006. "The transformation of the German financial system". *Revue d'économie politique* 116(4): 431. https://doi.org/10.3917/redp.164.0431.

Hall, C. 2019. "How the decline in community banks has hurt U.S. entrepreneurship". *Barrons*, 18 May; https://www.barrons.com/articles/how-the-decline-in-community-banks-has-hurt-u-s-entrepreneurship-51558184413.

Hall, P. & D. Soskice (eds) 2001. *Varieties of Capitalism: The Institutional Foundations of Comparative Advantage*. Oxford: Oxford University Press.

Hallerberg, M. & J. Markgraf 2018. "The corporate governance of public banks before and after the global financial crisis". *Global Policy* 9: 43–53.

Hardie, I. *et al.* 2013. "Banks and the false dichotomy in the comparative political economy of finance". *World Politics* 65(4): 691–728. https://doi.org/10.1017/S0043887113000221.

Hardie, I. & H. Thompson 2020. "Taking Europe seriously: European financialization and US monetary power". *Review of International Political Economy*, 1–19; https://doi.org/10.1080/09692290.2020.1769703.

Hau, H. & M. Thum 2009. "Subprime crisis and Board (in-)competence: private versus public banks in Germany". *Economic Policy* 24(60): 701–52.

Hay, C. 2002. *Political Analysis*. London: Palgrave Macmillan.

Henig, J., C. Hamnett & H. Feigenbaum 1988. "The politics of privatization: a comparative perspective". *Governance* 1(4): 442–68.

Henneke, H. 2019. *Kommunale Sparkassen: Verfassung und Organisation zwischen Selbstverwaltungsgarantie und Zentralisierungstrends: Darstellung*. Wiesbaden: Kommunal- und Schul-Verlag.

Herr, H. & Z. Nettekoven 2018. "The role of small and medium-sized enterprises in development: what can be learned from the German experience?" ILO Working Papers 53. Geneva: Global Labour University.

Hesse, M., C. Pauly & C. Reiermann 2012. "Auf konfrontationskurs; finanzmärkte: Minister Schäuble bremst bei der geplanten Bankenunion". *Der Spiegel*, 10 December.

Hilferding, R. 1910. *Das Finanzkapital. Eine Studie über die jüngste Entwicklung des Kapitalismus*. Wiener Volksbuchhandlung.

Hirschman, A. 2004. *Exit, Voice, and Loyalty: Responses to Decline in Firms, Organizations, and States*. Cambridge, MA: Harvard University Press.

Hoffmann, S. 2001. *Politics and Banking: Ideas, Public Policy, and the Creation of Financial Institutions*. Baltimore, MD: Johns Hopkins University Press.

Hoffmann, S. & M. Cassell 2010. *Mission Expansion in the Federal Home Loan Bank System*. Albany, NY: State University of New York Press.

Howarth, D. & L. Quaglia 2014. "Banking union as holy grail: rebuilding the single market in financial services, stabilizing Europe's banks and 'completing' Economic and Monetary Union". *JCMS: Journal of Common Market Studies* 51(S1), 103–23. https://doi.org/10.1111/jcms.12054.

Hüfner, F. 2010. "The German banking system: lessons from the financial crisis". OECD Economics Department Working Papers 788. Paris: OECD. https://doi.org/10.1787/5kmbm80pjkd6-en.

Hussam, S. 2018. *Public Banking for Infrastructure Finance*. Department of City and Regional Planning, Cornell University. http://www.rapidshift.net/public-banking-for-infrastructure-finance/.

Ioannidou, V. 2012. "A first step towards a banking union". Vox, 16 October; https://voxeu.org/article/first-step-towards-banking-union.

Jankowski, P. & Rickes 2018. *Die* Sparkassen-*Finanzgruppe – Deutschlands Champion bei der Finanzierung des Mittelstands*. Berlin: Deutscher Sparkassen- und Giroverband Abteilung Volkswirtschaft, Finanzmärkte und Wirtschaftspolitik.

Johnson, S. & J. Kwak 2011. *13 Bankers: The Wall Street Takeover and the Next Financial Meltdown*. New York: Vintage.

Jonietz, C., S. Mesch & A. Peters 2018. "Chancen und Herausforderungen der Digitalisierung in Banken und Sparkassen". In L. Fend & J. Hofmann (eds), *Digitalisierung in Industrie-, Handels- und Dienstleistungsunternehmen*, 367–82. Wiesbaden: Springer Fachmedien Wiesbaden.

Judd, J. & H. McGhee 2011. *Banking on America: How Main Street Partnership Banks Can Improve Local Economies*. Demos.

Judis, J. 2016. *The Populist Explosion: How the Great Recession Transformed American and European Politics*. Columbia Global Reports.

Junker, R. 1989. *The Bank of North Dakota: An Experiment in State Ownership*. McKinleyville, CA: Fithian Press.

Kaiser, A. 2015. "EU-Einlagesicherung: was deutsche Sparer jetzt wissen sollten". *Manager Magazin*, 25 November; https://www.manager-magazin.de/politik/europa/europaeische-einlagesicherung-will-die-eu-an-mein-sparbuch-a-1064400.html.

Kane, E. 1989. "How incentive-incompatible deposit-insurance funds fail". NBER Report w2836. Cambridge, MA: National Bureau of Economic Research. https://doi.org/10.3386/w2836.

Katz, B. & J. Nowak 2017. *The New Localism: How Cities Can Thrive in the Age of Populism*. Washington, DC: Brookings Institution Press.

Kelman, S. 2005. *Unleashing Change: A Study of Organizational Renewal in Government*. Washington, DC: Brookings Institution Press.

Kettl, D. 2018. *Politics of the Administrative Process*, seventh edition. Los Angeles, CA: Sage.

Khademian, A. 1992. *The SEC and Capital Market Regulation: The Politics of Expertise*. Pittsburgh, PA: University of Pittsburgh Press.

Khademian, A. 2002. *Working with Culture: How the Job Gets Done in Public Programs*. Washington, DC: CQ Press.

Klagge, B., R. Martin & P. Sunley 2017. "The spatial structure of the financial system and the funding of regional business: a comparison of Britain and Germany". In R. Martin & J. Pollard (eds), *Handbook on the Geographies of Money and Finance*, 125–55. Cheltenham: Elgar.

Klein, J. 2003. *Das Sparkassenwesen in Deutschland und Frankreich: Entwicklung, aktuelle Rechtsstrukturen und Möglichkeiten einer Annäherung*. Berlin: Duncker & Humblot.

Koch, P. *et al.* 2016. "The road ahead: perspectives on German banking". *German Banking Practice*, March. New York: McKinsey & Co.; https://www.mckinsey.com/~/media/McKinsey/Industries/Financial%20Services/Our%20Insights/The%20road%20ahead%20Perspectives%20on%20German%20banking/The-road-ahead-Perspectives-on-German-banking.ashx.

Kodryzcki, Y. & T. Elmated 2011. "The Bank of North Dakota: a model for Massachusetts and other states?" New England Public Policy Center Research Report 11–2. Federal Reserve Bank of Boston.

Köhler, M. 2011. "Naspa verliert 42 Millionen mit Lehman Papieren". *Frankfurter Allgemeine Zeitung*, 28 July; https://www.faz.net/-gzl-12mop.

Köhler, M. 2016. "The payout behaviour of German savings banks". Eurosystem Deutsche Bundesbank Discussion Paper 24. Frankfurt: Deutsche Bundesbank.

Köhler, P. 2004. "Oppositionsparteien planen Privatisierung der öffentlich-rechtlichen Kreditinstitute: CDU und FDP greifen Sparkassen an". *Handelsblatt*, 27 September.

Konzelmann, S. & M. Fovargue-Davies (eds) 2013. *Banking Systems in the Crisis: The Faces of Liberal Capitalism*. New York: Routledge.

Krahnen, J. & R. Schmidt (eds) 2004. *The German Financial System*. Oxford: Oxford University Press.

Kumkar, N. 2018. *The Tea Party, Occupy Wall Street, and the Great Recession*. Berlin: Springer International.

Kunz, A. 2018. "CDU und CSU haben großen Einfluss auf die Sparkassen". *Die Welt*, 17 June; https://www.welt.de/wirtschaft/article177676252/Parteien-haben-grossen-Einfluss-auf-die-Sparkassen.html.

Lane, C. 1995. *Industry and Society in Europe: Stability and Change in Britain, Germany, and France*. Cheltenham: Elgar.

Lane, J.-E. 2006. *Public Administration and Public Management: The Principal-Agent Perspective*. London: Routledge.

Lane, C. & S. Quack 1999. "The social dimensions of risk: bank financing of SMEs in Britain and Germany". *Organization Studies* 20(6): 987–1010.

La Porta, R., F. Lopez-De-Silanes & A. Shleifer 2002. "Government ownership of banks". *Journal of Finance* 57(1): 265–301.

Lazonick, W. 1991. *Business Organization and the Myth of the Market Economy*. Cambridge: Cambridge University Press.

Lessambo, F. 2020. "Public bank – Bank of North Dakota". In F. Lessamb (ed.), *The U.S. Banking System*, 139–55. Berlin: Springer International.

Lindenberg, C. 2019. Studie "Trusted Brands 2019": Umfrage: Allianz und Sparkassen genießen das größte Kundenvertrauen. *Das Investment*, 3 April; https://www.dasinvestment.com/studie-trusted-brands-2019-umfrage-allianz-und-Sparkassen-geniessen-das-groesste/.

Lukes, S. 2004. *Power: A Radical View*. Second edition. Basingstoke: Palgrave Macmillan.

Lütz, S. 2000. "From managed to market capitalism? German finance in transition". *German Politics* 9(2): 149–70.

Lütz, S. 2003. "Convergence within national diversity: a comparative perspective on the regulatory state in finance". MPIfG Discussion Paper 03/7. http://hdl.handle.net/10419/19901.

Macek, S. 2019. *White Paper: Public Banking in the Northeast and Midwest States*. Washington, DC: The Northeast-Midwest Institute.

Madrick, J. 2009. *The Case for Big Government*. Princeton, NJ: Princeton University Press.

Manager Magazin 2004. "Konsolidierung: 1000 Banken werden sterben". *Manager Magazin*, 7 December; https://www.manager-magazin.de/unternehmen/artikel/a-331512.html.

Markgraf, J. 2018. "Politicians as Bankers". *Hertie School of Governance Thesis*. Berlin: Hertie School of Governance.

Markgraf, J. & G. Rosas 2019. "On board with banks: do banking connections help politicians win elections?" *Journal of Politics* 81(4): 1357–70.

Marsden, P. 1981. "Introducing influence processes into a system of collective decisions". *American Journal of Sociology* 86(6), 1203–35.

Marshall, W. & L.-P. Rochon 2019. "Public banking and post-Keynesian economic theory". *International Journal of Political Economy* 48(1): 60–75. https://doi.org/10.1080/08911916.2018.1550947.

Mayer, U. 2019. "Rechnungshof-Kritik: Sparkassen geizen mit Gewinnausschüttung an Kommunen". Hessischer Rundfunk, 28 February; https://www.hessenschau.de/wirtschaft/rechnungshof-kritik-Sparkassen-geizen-mit-gewinnausschuettung-an-kommunen,rechnungshof-Sparkassen-100.html.

Merton, R. 1977. "An analytic derivation of the cost of deposit insurance and loan guarantees: an application of modern option pricing theory". *Journal of Banking & Finance* 1(1): 3–11. https://doi.org/10.1016/0378-4266(77)90015-2.

Milde, U. 2016. "Kleine Geldinstitute geraten unter Druck". *Leipziger Volkszeitung*, 11 October; https://www.lvz.de/Nachrichten/Wirtschaft/Wirtschaft-Regional/Kleine-Geldinstitute-geraten-unter-Druck.

Moe, R. 1987. "Exploring the limits of privatization". *Public Administration Review* 47(6): 453.

Moody's Investor Service 2018. "Sparkassen-Finanzgruppe". *Issuer In-Depth*. New York: Moody's Investor Service; https://www.dsgv.de/content/dam/dsgv-de/englische-inhalte/2018-04-savings-banks.pdfhttps://www.dsgv.de/content/dam/dsgv-de/englische-inhalte/2018-04-savings-banks.pdf.

Moore, P. 2017. "Low rates hobble Germany's public banks". *Euromoney*, 27 September; https://www.euromoney.com/article/b14xgzr4jxddnl/low-rates-hobble-germanys-public-banks.

Monopolkommission 2014. "Competition in the financial markets". *XXth Main Report of the Monopolies Commission*. Baden-Baden: Monopolkommission.

Moran, M. 2010. "The political economy of regulation: does it have any lessons for accounting research?" *Accounting and Business Research* 40(3): 215–25.

Morton, W. 1943. "Reviewed Work: *Branch Banking: Its Historical and Theoretical Position in America and Abroad* by John M. Chapman, Ray B. Westerfield, Gilbert E. Jackson, Maurice Megrah". *Accounting Review* 18(1): 80–82.

Müller, L. 2011. *Bank-Räuber: Wie kriminelle Manager und unfähige Politiker uns in den Ruin treiben*. Berlin: Econ.

Murinde, V., J. Agung & A. Mullineux 2004. "Patterns of corporate financing and financial system convergence in Europe". *Review of International Economics* 12(4): 693–705.

Mußler, H. 2014. "Staatsbanken in der Wagenburg". *Frankfurter Allgemeine Zeitung*, 7 September.

Mußler, H. 2015. Sparkassen-*Check: Die* Sparkassen *als Spielball der Politik*. 11 November; http://www.faz.net/1.3902948.

Netzel, W. (ed.) 2006. "Regionalgeschichte der Sparkassen-Finanzgruppe". Sparkassen in der Geschichte. Abt. 3, Forschung. Stuttgart: Deutscher Sparkassenverlag.

Newman, M. E. J. 2010. *Networks: An Introduction*. Oxford: Oxford University Press.

Niquette, M. & M. Sasso 2020. "U.S. doubles small-business loans' rate to 1% after lenders balk". *Washington Post*, 3 April; https://www.washingtonpost.com/business/on-small-business/us-doubles-small-business-loans-rate-to-1percent-after-lenders-balk/2020/04/02/c49c6d8a-752c-11ea-ad9b-254ec99993bc_story.html.

Niskanen, W. 1971. *Bureaucracy and Representative Government*. Chicago, IL: Aldine, Atherton.

Noack, H. 2009. "Back to the roots – Konsolidierung als kompetenter Partner der Sparkassen". In H. Noack & M. Schrooten (eds), *Die Zukunft der Landesbanken: Zwischen Konsolidierung und neuem Geschäftsmodell*, 5–19. Bonn: Friedrich-Ebert-Stiftung.

Noonan, L. 2017. "Germany's big banks profit from low interest rates". *Financial Times*, 26 July; https://www.ft.com/content/9afeaa18-707c-11e7-aca6-c6bd07df1a3c.

OECD 2014. *OECD Economic Surveys: Germany 2014*. https://www.oecd-ilibrary.org/content/publication/eco_surveys-deu-2014-en.

Ongena, S., G. Tümer-Alkan & N. von Westernhagen 2018. "Do exposures to sagging real estate, subprime, or conduits abroad lead to contraction and flight to quality in bank lending at home?" *Review of Finance* 22(4): 1335–73.

Osborne, D. & T. Gaebler 1992. *Reinventing Government: How the Entrepreneurial Spirit is Transforming the Public Sector*. New York: Plume.

Ordóñez, M. 2011. "The restructuring of the Spanish banking sector and the Royal Decree-Law for the reinforcement of the financial system"; https://www.bde.es/f/webbde/GAP/Secciones/SalaPrensa/InformacionInteres/ReestructuracionSectorFinanciero/Ficheros/en/mfo210211e.pdf.

O'Toole, Jr, L. 1997. "Treating networks seriously: practical and research-based agendas in public administration". *Public Administration Review* 57(1): 45–52.

Paár-Jákli, G. 2014. *Networked Governance and Transatlantic Relations: Building Bridges through Science Diplomacy*. New York: Routledge.

Pahnke, A. & F. Welter 2019. "The German Mittelstand: antithesis to Silicon Valley entrepreneurship?" *Small Business Economics* 52(2): 345–58. https://doi.org/10.1007/s11187-018-0095-4.

Paulick, J. 2010. "German-German monetary union caused economic shockwaves". *DW*, 18 September.

Peltz, J. 2019. "Public banks can be formed in California: Newsom signs new law". *Los Angeles Times*, 2 October; https://www.latimes.com/business/story/2019-10-02/public-banks-can-be-formed-under-bill-signed-by-newsom.

Pisani-Ferry, J. 2012. "The euro crisis and the new impossible trinity". Bruegel Policy Contribution.

Pizzo, S., M. Fricker & P. Muolo 1989. *Inside Job: The Looting of America's Savings and Loans*. New York: McGraw-Hill.

Plenarprotokoll 18/158 2016. (testimony of Deutscher Bundestag).

Pohl, H. 2005. "Die Sparkassen vom Ausgang des 19. Jahrhunderts bis zum Ende des Zweiten Weltkriegs". In H. Pohl, B. Rudolph & G. Schulz (eds), *Die Sparkassen vom Ausgang des 19. Jahrhunderts bis zum Ende des Zweiten Weltkriegs*, 21–64. Stuttgart: Deutscher Sparkassenverlag.

Pohl, H., B. Rudolph & G. Schulz (eds) 2005. "Wirtschafts- und Sozialgeschichte der deutschen Sparkassen im 20. Jahrhundert". Sparkassen *in der Geschichte. Forschung* 18. Stuttgart: Deutscher Sparkassenverlag.

Polsby, N. 1980. *Community Power and Political Theory: A Further Look at Problems of Evidence and Inference*. Second edition. New Haven, CT: Yale University Press.

Polster, A. 2005. "Savings bank reform in France: plus ca change, plus ca reste – presque – le meme". *Deutsche Bank Research, EU Monitor* 22. Frankfurt: Deutsche Bank.

Poppe, M. 2018. "Der große Vorteil der Sparkassen wird zur größten Gefahr für deutsche Wirtschaft". *FOCUS-Online*, 9 October; https://www.focus.de/finanzen/banken/enge-verbindungen-zur-politik-der-grosse-vorteil-der-Sparkassen-wird-nun-zur-groessten-gefahr-fuer-deutsche-wirtschaft_id_9723900.html?drucken=1.

Porter, M. 2003. "The economic performance of regions". *Regional Studies* 37(6/7): 549–78.

Powell, W. 1990. "Neither market nor hierarchy: network forms of organization". In B. Staw & L. Cummings (eds), *Research in Organizational Behaviour: An Annual Series of Analytical Essays and Critical Reviews*, Vol. 12: 295–336. Greenwich, CT: JAI Press.

Powell, W. & S. Grodal 2006. "Networks of innovators". In J. Fagerberg & D. Mowery (eds), *The Oxford Handbook of Innovation*, 56–85. Oxford: Oxford University Press.

Powers, J. 1969. "Branch versus unit banking: bank output and cost economies". *Southern Economic Journal* 36(2): 153.

PricewaterhouseCoopers 2012. "Millennials at work: reshaping the workplace in financial services". London: PricewaterhouseCoopers; https://www.pwc.com/gx/en/financial-services/publications/assets/pwc-millenials-at-work.pdf.

Public Banking Institute 2020. "Legislations and Local Groups by State".
https://www.publicbankinginstitute.org/.

Quinlan, B. 2017. "Industry woes on the rise". *International Banker*, 12 March;
https://internationalbanker.com/banking/industry-woes-rise/.

Randow, J. & A. Kirchfeld 2010. "Germany's Mittelstand still thrives". *Business Week*,
4 October; https://web.archive.org/web/20101004130646/http://www.businessweek.
com/globalbiz/content/sep2010/gb20100929_905740.htm.

Reyes, E. 2019. "Wesson puts municipal bank back on table". *Los Angeles Times*, 14 October.

Ruckdäschel, S. 2015. *Leadership of Networks and Performance*. Wiesbaden: Springer
Fachmedien Wiesbaden.

Sachse, J. 2016. "Die Kommunen werden ärmer – und ihre Sparkassen immer fetter".
Frankfurter Allgemeine Zeitung, 9 November; https://correctiv.org/aktuelles/
Sparkassen/2016/11/09/die-kommunen-werden-aermer-und-ihre-Sparkassen-
immer-fetter/.

Sachse, J. & L. Weigner 2016. "Deutschlands Sparkassen sind großzügig beim Spenden –
und knausrig bei den Ausschüttungen an die Kommunen". *Correctiv.org*, 10 November;
https://correctiv.org/aktuelles/Sparkassen/2016/11/10/deutschlands-Sparkassen-sind-
grosszuegig-beim-spenden-und-knausrig-bei-den-ausschuettungen-an-die-kommunen/.

Sackmann, C. 2018. "Keine Ahnung, aber fürstlich bezahlt: Wie Lokalpolitiker Sparkassen
kontrollieren". *FOCUS-Online*, 19 June; https://www.focus.de/finanzen/banken/laien-
mit-parteibuch-keine-ahnung-aber-fuerstlich-bezahlt-wie-lokalpolitiker-Sparkassen-
kontrollieren_id_9116995.html?drucken=1.

Schackmann-Fallis, K.-P., H. Gischer & M. Weiß 2017. "A case for boring banking and
re-intermediation". *Faculty of Economics and Management Working Paper* 18/2017.
Magdeburg: Otto von Guericke Universität Magdeburg.

Schattschneider, E. 1975. *The Semisovereign People: A Realist's View of Democracy in
America*. Boston, MA: Dryden Press.

Scherrer, C. 2014. "Öffentliche banken im sog der finanzialisierung". In M. Heires &
A. Nölke (eds), *Politische Ökonomie der Finanzialisierung*, 147–61. Wiesbaden: Springer
Fachmedien Wiesbaden.

Scherrer, C. (ed.) 2017. *Public Banks in the Age of Financialization: A Comparative
Perspective*. Northampton, MA: Elgar.

Schieritz, M. 2012. "Wer hütet die Banken?" *Die Zeit Online*, 13 September.

Schilling, M. & C. Phelps 2007. "Interfirm collaboration networks: the impact of large-scale
network structure on firm innovation". *Management Science* 53(7): 1113–26.

Schmalzl, J. & F. Wiegand 2019. "Standortbestimmung digitalisierung Sparkassen". *BaFin
Perspektiven* 1/2019. Berlin: Deutscher Sparkassen- und Giroverband e.V; https://www.
dsgv.de/positionen/fokuspapiere/standortbestimmung-digitalisierung-Sparkassen.html

Schmidt, R., H. Seibel & P. Thomes 2016. *From Microfinance to Inclusive Banking: Why
Local Banking Works*. Weinheim: Wiley-VCH.

Schmidt, T. & L. Zwick 2012. *In Search for a Credit Crunch in Germany*. Bochum: RWI.

Schneiberg, M. 2013. "Lost in transposition? (A cautionary tale): the Bank of North Dakota
and prospects for reform in American Banking". In M. Lounsbury & E. Boxenbaum
(eds), *Institutional Logics in Action, Part A: Vol. 39 Part A*, 277–310. Bingley: Emerald.

Schreiber, M. 2018. "Allzu große Nähe". *Süddeutsche.de*, 14 January; https://www.
sueddeutsche.de/wirtschaft/Sparkassen-allzu-grosse-naehe-1.3824744.

Schroeder, P. 2017. "Banks spent record amounts on lobbying in recent election". *Reuters*,
8 March; https://www.reuters.com/article/us-usa-banks-lobbying-idUSKBN16F26P.

Schulz, A. 2010. "Wir brauchen einen besseren Staat und zugleich gesunde Banken und
Marktstrukturen". *Zeitschrift Für Das Gesamte Kreditwesen*, 1 December.

Schrooten, M. 2009. "*Landesbanken*: Zukunft Ungewiss". *Wirtschaftsdienst* 89(10): 666–71.

Seikel, D. 2013. *Der Kampf um öffentlich-rechtliche Banken: Wie die Europäische Kommission Liberalisierung durchsetzt*. Frankfurt: Campus Verlag.

Semenyshyn, H. 2017. "Marginalizing the German savings banks through the European Single Market". In C. Scherrer (ed.), *Public Banks in the Age of Financialization*, 176–92. Cheltenham: Elgar.

Shleifer, A. & R. Vishny 1994. "Politicians and firms". *Quarterly Journal of Economics* 109(4): 995–1025.

Shonfield, A. 1968. *Modern Capitalism: The Changing Balance of Public and Private Power*. Oxford: Oxford University Press.

Siclari, D. (ed.) 2015. *Italian Banking and Financial Law: Regulating Activities*. Basingstoke: Palgrave Macmillan.

Siemens, A. 2008. "Auch Sparkassen haben sich verzockt". *FOCUS Online*, 5 November; https://www.focus.de/finanzen/boerse/finanzkrise/finanzkrise-auch-Sparkassen-haben-sich-verzockt_aid_346401.html.

Simon, H. 2017. "Why Germany still has so many middle-class manufacturing jobs". *Harvard Business Review*, 2 May; https://hbr.org/2017/05/why-germany-still-has-so-many-middle-class-manufacturing-jobs.

Simpson, C. 2013. *The German Sparkassen (Savings Banks): A Commentary and a Case Study*. London: Civitas.

Smyser, W. 1993. *The German Economy: Colossus at the Crossroads*. Second edition. New York: St Martin's Press.

Spiegel Wirtschaft 2016. Sparkassen *planen Kampagne gegen europäische Einlagensicherung*. 6 May; https://www.spiegel.de/wirtschaft/soziales/Sparkassen-kampagne-gegen-europaeische-einlagensicherung-a-1091072.html.

Spiegel Online 2016. "Entscheidung der Aufsicht: StadtSparkasse verliert Streit um Gewinne gegen Düsseldorf". *Spiegel Online*, 9 June; https://www.spiegel.de/wirtschaft/unternehmen/stadtSparkasse-duesseldorf-verliert-streit-um-gewinne-gegen-oberbuergermeister-a-1096787.html.

Spiegel Online 2019. "Digitalisierung: Banken haben seit 2014 jede fünfte Filiale geschlossen". *Spiegel Online*, 4 June; https://www.spiegel.de/wirtschaft/unternehmen/banken-haben-seit-2014-jede-fuenfte-filiale-geschlossen-a-1270814.html.

Staff 2016. "Mehr Girokonten für Flüchtlinge; Sparkasse Nürnberg zählt schon 2000 Asylbewerber als Kunden". *Nürnberger Nachrichten*, 17 February.

Stefan, G. & F.-M. Jorge 2018. "Governance, cohesion and banking in Spain from a spatial perspective". *Safe Bank* 2(71): 7–29. https://doi.org/10.26354/bb.1.2.71.2018.

Stern, K. 1984. "Sparkassen und Kommunen. Ihre kommunal- und Sparkassenrechtliche Verknüpfung". In Deutscher Sparkassen- und Giroverband (ed.), *Standortbestimmung. Entwicklungslinien der deutschen Kreditwirtschaft*. Stuttgart: Deutscher Sparkassen.

Stevens, G. & L. Steinauser 2013. "Sparkassen lassen in Europa die Muskeln spielen". *Wall Street Journal*, 11 November; https://www.wsj.com/articles/Sparkassen-lassen-in-europa-die-muskeln-spielen-1384164105.

Stevenson, B. & J. Wolfers 2011. *Trust in Public Institutions over the Business Cycle*. National Bureau of Economic Research. https://doi.org/10.3386/w16891.

Storbeck, O. 2018. "Germany's *Landesbanken* still seeking clean bill of health". *Financial Times*, 2 November; https://www.ft.com/content/d7d380cc-dcdb-11e8-9f04-38d397e6661c.

Storbeck, O. 2019. "'Sticky' savings banks keep big German rivals in check". *Financial Times*, 24 April; https://www.ft.com/content/5f44426e-5ac5-11e9-9dde-7aedca0a081a.

Streeck, W. 1992. *Social Institutions and Economic Performance: Studies of Industrial Relations in Advanced Capitalist Economies*. London: Sage.

Streeck, W. & P. Schmitter (eds) 1985. *Private Interest Government: Beyond Market and State*. London: Sage.

Strotmann, A. 2019. "Der Sparkassen-Bus rollt jetzt durch Düsseldorf". *Westdeutsche Zeitung*, 2 September; https://www.wz.de/nrw/duesseldorf/Sparkasse-setzt-in-duesseldorf-mit-bus-auf-mobile-filiale_aid-45544893.

Suleiman, E. & J. Waterbury 2019. *The Political Economy of Public Sector Reform and Privatization*. New York: Routledge.

Sydow, J. *et al.* 2011. "A silent cry for leadership: organizing for leading (in) clusters". *Leadership Quarterly* 22(2): 328–43.

Tadayon, A. 2017. "Oakland public bank organizers look to fund renewable energy". *The East Bay Times*, 6 October.

Thelen, K. 2007. "Contemporary challenges to the German vocational training system". *Regulation & Governance* 1(3): 247–60.

Tilly, R. 1980. *Kapital, Staat und sozialer Protest in der deutschen Industrialisierung: Ges. Aufsätze*. Gottingen: Vandenhoeck & Ruprecht.

Timmler, V. 2016. "Basis zum Arbeiten; Banken verweigern vielen anerkannten Asylbewerbern ein Konto, weil diese keine lukrativen Kunden sind. Bald wird ein Gesetz sie dazu zwingen". *Süddeutsche Zeitung*, 29 January.

Tischer, M. 2011. *Effizienzmessung im Sparkassensektor am Beispiel regionaler Cluster*. Sternenfels: Verl. Wiss. & Praxis.

Tullock, G. 1987. *The Politics of Bureaucracy*. Lanham, MD: University Press of America.

Tversky, A. & D. Kahneman 1992. "Advances in prospect theory: cumulative representation of uncertainty". *Journal of Risk and Uncertainty* 5(4): 297–323.

Ufer, T. 2017. "The millennial turnover problem in the financial services industry". Hppy, 1 December; https://gethppy.com/employee-turnover/the-millennial-turnover-problem-in-the-financial-services-industry.

United States 2011. *The Financial Crisis Inquiry Report: Final Report of the National Commission on the Causes of the Financial and Economic Crisis in the United States*. Public Affairs.

Uzzi, B. 1996. "The sources and consequences of embeddedness for the economic performance of organizations: the network effect". *American Sociological Review* 61(4): 674.

van Meerhaeghe, M. 2006. "Bismarck and the social question". *Journal of Economic Studies* 33(4): 284–301.

Vitols, S. 1998. "Are German banks different?" *Small Business Economics* 10(2): 79–91.

Vitols, S. 2005. "Changes in Germany's bank-based financial system: implications for corporate governance". *Corporate Governance: An International Review* 13(3): 386–96.

Weber, M. 1964. *The Theory of Social and Economic Organization*. New York: Free Press.

Wehler, H. 2006. *Deutsche Gesellschaftsgeschichte. Bd. 3: Von der "Deutschen Doppelrevolution" bis zum Beginn des Ersten Weltkrieges: 1849 – 1914*. München: Beck.

Welp, C. 2011. "Unbeachtetes Risiko: Sparkassen bieten trügerische Sicherheit". *Handelsblatt Online*, 21 March; https://www.handelsblatt.com/finanzen/banken-versicherungen/unbeachtetes-risiko-Sparkassen-bieten-truegerische-sicherheit/4220878.html.

Wenus, L. 2020. "S.F. lays groundwork for public bank to wrest money from Wall Street". *San Francisco Public Press*, 18 January.

Westerlund, M. 2010. "Learning and innovation in inter-organizational network collaboration". *Journal of Business & Industrial Marketing* 25(6): 435–42.

Williamson, O. 1994. "Visible and invisible governance". *American Economic Review* 84(2): 323–6.

Wilmarth Jr., A. 2015. "A two-tiered system of regulation is needed to preserve the viability of community banks and reduce the risks of megabanks". *Michigan State Law Review* 249: 249–370.

Wilson, J. 2000. *Bureaucracy: What Government Agencies Do and Why They Do It*. New York: Basic Books.

Woodrow, W. 1887. "Study of administration". *Political Science Quarterly* 2(2): 197–222.

Wissenschaftsförderung der Sparkassen-Finanzgruppe e.V. 2011. "*Zeiten & Perspektiven Bilder und Texte zur Geschichte der* Sparkassen". Stuttgart: Dt. Sparkassen-Verl.

Wysocki, J. & H.-G. Günther (eds) 1998. "Geschichte der Sparkassen in der DDR: 1945 bis 1990". Sparkassen *in der Geschichte Abt. 3, Forschung* 8. Stuttgart: Dt. Sparkassenverl.

Zysman, J. 1994. *Governments, Markets, and Growth: Financial Systems and the Politics of Industrial Change*. Ithaca, NY: Cornell University Press.

INDEX

Note: numbers in brackets preceded by *n* refer to notes.